D1453642

THE GUIDEBOOK FOR THE STUDY OF PSYCHICAL RESEARCH

THE GUIDEBOOK FOR THE STUDY OF
PSYCHICAL RESEARCH

Robert H. Ashby

SAMUEL WEISER, INC.
New York

1973

For Jenny and Mrs. P.

who made this book possible

First Published 1972
Revised Printing 1973

Published by
SAMUEL WEISER, INC.
734 Broadway
New York, New York 10003

ISBN 0-87728-188-2

Library of Congress Catalogue Card No. 72-78575

Printed in U.S.A. by
NOBLE OFFSET PRINTERS, INC.
NEW YORK, N.Y. 10003

THE GUIDEBOOK FOR THE STUDY OF PSYCHICAL RESEARCH

Robert H. Ashby

Table of Contents

PREFACE

This book is intended for the person interested in Extrasensory Perception (ESP) and related topics who determines to investigate psychical research. I have written it because during the years of my involvement in the field, I have often been approached by people who are genuinely concerned about ESP and an invariable question is, "How do I find out about such matters?" They have wanted to know which books they should read; where there were libraries with substantial collections on the subject; which bookshops specialized in works dealing with the topics of psychical research; which organizations were devoted to psychical research or connected issues and how they could join such groups. There have often been queries regarding mediums: what exactly is a medium? how does one find a medium? how does one deal with a medium in a sitting? and how does one judge the quality of a medium and the significance of the mediumistic material from a sitting?

It is obvious that the beginning student of psychical research needs some guidance as to where and how to proceed with his studies, and those who already have some knowledge of the field need to decide at which point to undertake further study of a very puzzling mass of data, interpretations, theories, and disagreements. It is in the hope of helping to meet these needs that this volume has been prepared.

In response to the rapidly growing interest in ESP, there is a definite improvement in library holdings concerning psychical research. There has been a spate of volumes dealing with ESP during the last few years, and the serious student of the discipline may well be confused as to the relative merit, seriousness of purpose, and soundness of scholarship behind many of these popular treatments. Because of this difficulty, I have prepared in Chapters II and III two separate annotated bibliographies. The first is a list of approximately forty books which should prove useful for those without previous experience in studying psychical research. The second of approximately forty books is for the student who has learned the basic facts and procedures of the discipline and feels that he is ready to proceed into more complex issues and deeper, more subtle discussions. Works in both chapters have been grouped according to major topics and coverage. They are, of course, of varying difficulty and I have tried to indicate something about this in the annotations.

In addition to the annotated works, in both chapters I have listed a considerable number of other books which I feel are worth consulting. I did not wish to make the bibliographies either exhaustive or exhausting. They are merely possible and, I believe, sound starting points for the student. His own particular interests will then lead him on to further reading. The information in the bibliographies is as accurate as I could determine; however, readers may well find that some important books are no longer in print or that they are available only in a hardback or only in a paperback edition.

I am grateful to Dr. J. B. Rhine and the Editor of *The Journal of Parapsychology* for their kind permission to use some of the Glossary definitions from their publication. The two quotations from SCIENCE DIGEST are reprinted with the permission of SCIENCE DIGEST,© The Hearst Corporation. I have benefitted greatly from the sound criticism and constructive suggestions given by Miss Renée Haynes, Mrs. Rosalind Heywood, and Mrs. Ena Twigg. Mr. Leslie Price has been of enormous assistance in clarifying bibliographical points and in gaining information about library holdings. The staff of The College of Psychic Studies have been most cooperative and patient with my use of their fine library; my appreciation also goes to Mrs. Laura F. Knipe of The American Society for Psychical Research and to Mrs. G. Babusis of the Eileen J. Garrett Library at The Parapsychology Foundation for their assistance. Finally, in this undertaking, as in all, my wife's constant encouragement, understanding, and perceptive suggestions have been indispensable.

For the opinions expressed and any errors I am, of course, solely responsible.

Robert H. Ashby

CHAPTER ONE

THE NATURE OF PSYCHICAL RESEARCH

There is surely no field of study in which the concepts, beliefs, and biases of our "common sense" world clash so violently with the data collected and analyzed by scholars as psychical research or, as it is frequently termed today, parapsychology. Nor is there any discipline which aims at following the scientific methods whose data and theories are so widely disclaimed by orthodox scientists. Indeed, a sizeable majority of scientists would doubtless contend that psychical researchers have not established that there is anything to investigate. In short, the scientific community at large still rejects the data that indicate that "paranormal phenomena"—earlier called "psychic phenomena"—i.e., occurrences which do not fit into currently known patterns, behavior, or theories, ever occur. Dr. George R. Price may be cited as typical of this school of thought. He is quoted in *Science Digest* for November, 1965, as saying:

> My opinion concerning parapsychologists is that many of them are dependent on clerical and statistical errors and unintentional use of sensory clues, and that all extra-chance results not so explicable are dependent on deliberate fraud or mildly abnormal mental conditions. [1]

Such a situation in scientific circles, following ninety years of careful research into psychic phenomena might be termed a paranormal phenomenon itself. It is, however, true that this attitude has gradually changed during the last twenty-five years and that an increasing number of younger scientists in many fields are open-minded about Extrasensory Perception (ESP) and feel that psychical research is an important area of study. The changing climate of opinion was indicated in a most encouraging manner in December of 1969 when the American Association for the Advancement of Science accepted The Parapsychological Association as an affiliate member.

Why has this fledgling science aroused such scientific hostility and skepticism? The scientific method utilized in scientific disciplines can be summarized as one in which the phenomenon under study must meet the following criteria:

1. isolation from other phenomena in nature

2. observation under conditions controlled by the scientist

3. repeated experimentation

4. results both statistically assessable and obtainable by any other scientist replicating the experiment and its conditions precisely

Thus, one must have: isolation, observation, control, ex-

1 "See, however, his letter to the Editor of *Science,* January 28, 1972, retracting his charge of 1955 that Rhine and Soal were guilty of fraud."

perimentation, measureable data, and repeatability both of experimentation and of results in order to establish the reality of the phenomenon. It is true, of course, that this method is more readily applied with some types of phenomena than others. Chemistry and astronomy cannot be approached in exactly the same manner; and behavioral sciences like psychology have had to modify the methodology somewhat. Nevertheless, these canons of evidentiality and predictability undergird the acceptance of phenomena by the scientific community.

The central problem is that paranormal phenomena have very rarely conformed to this pattern. They have most often been "spontaneous," occurring without prior planning or preparation for observation, control, or experimentation. In such instances, researchers have had to depend upon witnesses to the phenomena to describe what they believe occurred as carefully as possible, and as soon as possible after the "ostensibly paranormal" phenomenon occurred. The phrase "ostensibly paranormal" is used to show that whether the experience was, in fact, paranormal is a judgement to be made *only* after all of the evidence has been analyzed and all "normal" explanations have had to be rejected. Many critics of psychical research may not fully realize how many reports of strange happenings have been proven by parapsychologists to be explicable by perfectly normal means, or have been rejected as inadequately supported by convincing evidence. Probably few more than one out of a hundred reports received have ever been found worthy of publication.

Such witnessed accounts of phenomena possibly paranormal in nature do not satisfy the scientist as meeting either his usual methods or his standards of evidence. Hence, parapsychologists set out to devise experiments which would conform to the scientific method. While there were numerous earlier attempts, it is during the last forty years, beginning in the United States with Dr. J. B. Rhine at Duke University, that researchers in many countries have conducted such controlled laboratory experiments and have garnered impressive evidence that ESP does occur under controlled conditions, that these experiments can be repeated by other researchers, and can sometimes yield similar extra-chance results.

These experiments have centered upon using a pack of test cards consisting of twenty-five cards with five different designs. The person trying to demonstrate ESP, the "subject," would try to guess which card was being held by the experimenter in another part of the room, another room, or another building. Since there are five cards of each of the five designs in the pack, the chance result would be one out of five, or five right in the pack of twenty-five. If a subject could obtain appreciably more than five right in each test over a considerable number of tests, this showed that something other than chance was operating; and since there was no opportunity for the subject to use his five senses to ascertain the correct card, there was sound statistical evidence to indicate that "something" other than chance and other than the five senses was responsible for the accurate "guessing." That "something" has been termed Extrasensory Perception.

Dr. Helmut Schmidt, formerly a physicist with the Boeing Scientific Research Laboratories and successor to Dr. J. B. Rhine as Director of The Foundation for Research into the Nature of Man, caused a sensation by publishing in 1969 and subsequently precognitive and PK results of experiments conducted with randomness assured by using "single quantum processes". Subjects tried to guess which of four bulbs would next light and indicated their choice by pressing the appropriate button. Three subjects performed a total of over 63,000 trials with precognitive success at odds of two billion to one against chance. In a second test of 20,000 trials, subjects could choose either to press the button of a lamp that would light or one that would not, and the results were equally impressive. The scientific community seems to have been more impressed by Dr. Schmidt's work than that of any other parapsychologist of recent years; and his sophisticated use of highly complex technology to guarantee both randomness and accuracy of recording results is an important development.

Yet, despite this statistical evidence, many scientists still reject the reality of ESP. Why? First, because, as Dr. Price said, there *could* be errors made by the researchers in recording the results of the tests, and because of the researchers's bias in favor of ESP, such errors would tend to support rather than to deny it. Second, where the researcher and the subject were close, it *might* be possible that the subject had "sensory clues," i. e., heard the researcher inadvertently mumble the name of the design on the card, or saw through a badly printed card and so learned which design was being held, or noticed that the researcher tended to act in a particular way when a certain design came up in the pack. Third, since we do not know a great deal about how we learn, there *may* be a perfectly physical explanation which is possibly "mildly abnormal" or unusual, but still within the sensory system. Last, there *might* be "deliberate fraud" either by the subject or the researcher or both. Obviously, one cannot absolutely refute such an allegation unless one were present during all the experiments and observed both parties involved very carefully; even then, of course, by another scientist, one could be suspected of fraudulent conspiracy with the original two, and so on *ad infinitum*. In short, the accusation of fraud is impossible to disprove completely, however honest and meticulous a researcher has been. But one may fairly ask, what would either the researcher or the subject gain by such fraud? Certainly not financial rewards: there is very little money available for research, and most subjects have been volunteers; possibly fame either as a scholar or as a gifted psychic, but such reputations have more generally been viewed as notoriety than renown in the scientific community; possibly self-esteem, but this would be absurd since the fraudulent person would know better than anyone that he was a fraud. It is most difficult to see what end would be served by such alleged collusion. It assumes either dishonesty or *naïveté* to an extraordinary degree over decades by hundreds of intelligent and responsible people who had no reason to cheat; but it remains the final, unanswerable criticism which has been faced by psychical researchers for ninety years.

The scientists have issued those criticisms partly because they found that the experiments described above did not prove so repeatable or so conclusive in terms of results as Dr. Rhine and his associates claimed. Why? The enormous amount of research during the last twenty-five years into the psychological states conducive to the operation of ESP has established firmly that this faculty (generally termed "*psi*" and covering all aspects of the paranormal ability) is elusive, unpredictable, emotionally triggered and repressed, sensitive to surroundings, conditions, and, especially, to attitudes towards psi itself. Psi is much more likely to operate if the subject and the researcher are predisposed to believe that psi does or may exist, and if both the conditions and the experimenters are relaxed, comfortable, and cheerful. Parapsychologists have found that some subjects perform better with certain researchers than with others; that results depend upon the subject's health and mental state; that subjects tend to lose interest in the numerous repeats of the test and boredom suppresses psi; and that many other generally uncontrollable variables can affect the performance of psi.

Now for a scientist to achieve the kinds of results which seem to demonstrate statistically that psi does exist, it is clear that he would need something other than the detached, skeptical frame of mind with which he prides himself he approaches his experiments. He might need different surroundings from the sterile, utilitarian, stark laboratory; he must hope that he could establish a warm rapport with the subject; he must realize that if the subject was distraught in some way, psi might well not evidence itself; and he must recognize that most of these variables he could not control. In short, it appears that to establish for himself psi as a reality, the scientist must already believe, partially at least, that it *could* exist. This has proven too much of a departure for most scientists, and it is not surprising that their attempts to repeat Rhine's experiments have not been generally successful. And so they have gathered far less evidence of psi than psychical researchers when, for conviction, they have needed far more. Psychologist Ernest R. Hilgard explains why in *Science Digest,* November, 1965:

> To demonstrate something highly implausible requires better evidence than to demonstrate something plausible. The reason is that supporting evidence for the plausible finding comes from many directions, while the implausible one must hang from the slender thread of nonrandomness until certain systematic relationships are found that tie it firmly to what is known.

Despite the widespread denial of the reality of psi by the scientific community, psychical research continues amidst rapidly growing interest in its findings and its significance among the general public. This is because *if* psi and its manifestations do exist a revolution in general scientific and "common sense" thinking will be necessary. Psychical researchers ask whether some people can:

exchange ideas via some extrasensory means termed "telepathy"? If so, does this indicate anything about the extent of the mind's powers and range?

perceive objects, persons, or happenings without the use of the five senses, sometimes at great distances? If so, does "clairvoyance" demonstrate anything about the nature of man's perceptions?

foresee events in detail without any inferential or logical reasons? If so, does this "precognition" signify anything about man's free will?

apparently "step back in time"? If so, does this "retrocognition" indicate anything about the quality, or even the existence, of time itself?

perceive accurate visions of persons known and unknown, alive and dead? If so, do these veridical "apparitions" mean anything in terms of man's dramatic faculties, or possibly of his basic essence, the so-called "soul"?

cause objects to move without touching, pushing, or throwing them in any normal manner which science considers necessary by the laws of motion? If so, does this "telekinesis," "psychokinesis," or "PK" demonstrate anything about the power of thought or human will?

perceive detailed data about an unknown person by touching objects once in that person's possession? If so, does this "psychometry" show anything about the tactile faculty and about any normally imperceptible residue of an intimate and unique character upon an object which the sensitive's fingers seem to detect?

communicate with "personalities" which claim to be, and sometimes seem to be, the spirits of deceased persons? If so, does this "discarnate communication" indicate anything about death and the possible survival of human personality?

Do a whole range of other ostensibly paranormal phenomena occur, including "poltergeists," dream phenomena, animal phenomena, "apports," "materializations" by means of a strange substance termed "ectoplasm," "table tipping" wherein the table seems to move of itself and to tap out meaningful messages, "levitation," wherein an object or a person seems to rise without any known means of doing so, "astral projection" or "out-of-the-body experiences" wherein the percipient claims to have left his physical body and while in his "astral body" to have perceived persons, places, and events which he could not have perceived normally from the location of his physical body, and "spiritual healing"? If so, do such phenomena shed any light upon the scientific framework within which we usually move and think?

In view of such questions and the documentation gathered since the close of the last century which suggests that some of these things do happen on occasion, it is hardly surprising that the scientific establishment has not reacted kindly to psychical research. Yet, as Dr. Rhine has pointed out, it is surely unscientific to term something "impossible," especially in the face of the extant evidence available for careful and critical scrutiny. Unfortunately, far too few scientists have examined the evidence in such a manner. The prevalent attitude has very often been that of the Cambridge don of chemistry who, in debating the reality of psychic phenomena with Sir Arthur Conan Doyle, based his rejection of their actuality upon the fact that "I once attended a séance." Doyle retorted that were he to debate a topic in chemistry, how absurd his position would be were he to base his conclusions on the statement, "I once visited a chemistry laboratory."

It is apparent that the establishment of psi as a reality has posed very real problems during the ninety years of psychical research and that its occurrence remains a matter of considerable controversy. And within psychical research itself there is disagreement as to the liklihood of different types of phenomena. Few parapsychologists today are convinced about most so-called "physical phenomena" which flourished in the last half of the nineteenth and the first quarter of the twentieth centuries. This category includes such things as materializations of "spirit forms" which were claimed to be composed of an unknown, semi-physical substance termed "ectoplasm" by the distinguished French phsyiologist Charles Richet; "apports," or small objects such as stones, flowers, or even small animals which seemed to appear at a séance without any normal means of doing so; "levitation" of objects and people, as quite a few researchers and laymen claimed to have witnessed, sometimes in good light, especially as performed by the most remarkable medium of all, Dunglas Home; "psychic" or "spirit" photography in which faces and forms of deceased persons would appear on the photograph, supposedly without any normal means of doing so; and a whole spectrum of strange happenings occurring in the dark or semi-dark, which the psychics—termed "physical mediums"—insisted was essential because "ectoplasm" was generally allergic both to light and to touch by any witness.

The principal reasons for the widespread doubt as to the reality of such physical phenomena are first, that virtually every physical medium was disclosed at some point in his career to have produced fraudulent phenomena, and these disclosures naturally placed in doubt al' the other phenomena produced: were they genuinely paranormal or also fraudulent? Second, very few physical mediums ever agreed to scientific examination under conditions controlled by the researcher (although there have been some remarkable exceptions to this statement); and, third, such phenomena seem extremely rare today, when the techniques of investigating such claims are greatly ·advanced over those available when such phenomena flourished. Whether this present rarity of physical mediums is due to the greater risk of detection in fraud or to some other reason is not certain.

There is far better evidence that "poltergeists" (literally, German for "noisy spirits"), termed Recurrent Spontaneous Psychokinesis or RSPK by parapsychologists, do, in fact, occur. The large number of well-attested instances of strange movements of objects in full light, odd noises in houses, sudden feelings of a cold breeze, etc., precludes hoax or imagination as the only explanations. However, some parapsychologists feel that such phenomena can be explained in many, if not all, cases by such causes as underground water, rats, mice, youthful pranks, and overly active imagination. It is interesting that in such poltergeist manifestations, there is generally a child near the age of puberty present and that the phenomena seem to center around the adolescent. Whether, in a genuinely paranormal instance, there is intentional use by the adolescent of some psychokinetic faculty to make objects move, or whether there is a completely unconscious use of such an ability remains a matter of doubt and controversy. Since poltergeists are location centered, the investigator can rarely observe the phenomena under laboratory conditions, but delicate recording devices, motion picture cameras, and other equipment enable the modern parapsychologist to investigate thoroughly such RSPK reports. And some of the adolescents who have been at the psychic vortex of such phenomena have been found in laboratory tests to be gifted with a strong psi faculty.

While poltergeist phenomena do not lend themselves to laboratory experimentation, PK has. Dr. Rhine and other researchers have conducted lengthy experiments over a considerable number of years to see whether subjects in the laboratory under controlled conditions could "will" dice to fall a certain way; and statistical evidence that PK has operated has been published. It is interesting to note that subjects attempting to demonstrate PK have been tested at various distances from the dice and, generally, the results have been in accordance with the individual subject's belief as to whether distance has any effect on PK: i. e., a subject who thought it did not matter would score just as well twenty feet from the dice as one foot away; one who believed the opposite declined in score as his distance increased. This shows again the bearing of belief upon the psi faculty. The acceptance of such evidence among parapsychologists has been mixed: replication of the results has not been easy or frequent, giving rise to doubt among some that the case for PK has been statistically proven.

The other large category of the paranormal, besides the physical, is termed "mental," and this has received by far the greatest attention during the last forty years of research. Under this heading would come telepathy, clairvoyance, precognition, retrocognition, and mediumistic communications. Psychometry and apparitions seem to span the two general categories of physical and mental: whether the object the psychometrist handles actually does contain a "psychic residue" from its possessor which the psychometrist perceives by handling it or whether the object acts merely as a catalyst or focal point for his own psi faculty is not yet clear. Thus psychometry may be entirely mental or partially mental and partially physical in nature. Similarly with apparitions: is the verifiable figure and/or scene which is perceived by the witness a spatial one, that is, is "something there" in an objective sense, as when one perceives a table in the middle of the room; or is the apparition a "veridical hallucination," that is, a mentally constructed and projected image really "seen within" but *seeming* to be "outside" one, hence not objective but subjective in nature? The theoretical difficulties inherent in apparitions pose one of the most fascinating and complex problems in psychical research.

Within mental phenomena there are divisions between spontaneous, experimental, and mediumistic data. The first yields documentary evidence which must be assessed in terms of the quality and quantity of the witnesses, the time lapse between the occurrence and the report, the possibility of normal explanations, such as subconscious memory, logical inference based upon known but consciously forgotten information, discrepancies between accounts, elaborations due to dramatic tendencies, faulty memory, poor light, or fraud. It can well be appreciated that a perfect case in which the evidence passes every such criterion with flying colors is so rare as to be virtually nonexistent: one can always find some flaw in human testimony. But if researchers can gather thousands of such accounts from a wide variety of countries and cultures, covering the entire spectrum of ages, social, economic, religious, and political types and predilections over a period of almost a century; and if these accounts when closely analyzed disclose striking similarities in characteristics—both in terms of what they include and what they exclude—then, even if individually there are flaws in each, the cumulative effect of such a collection can be most impressive, and to many, convincing. This latter viewpoint is often called the "faggot theory," meaning that while each stick within a bundle may be easily broken (flawed), when bound together with a great many others, the joint strength withstands such an attack.

As we have seen, however, spontaneous phenomena are neither repeatable at will, statistically measurable, controllable, nor entirely free of human bias and error of observation. Also, such phenomena are difficult to categorize because each is unique in terms of its time, place, and conditions of occurrence. Consequently, a great many different interpretations of these accounts are possible. While these phenomena are very frequently of a lasting importance and conviction to those who participated in or witnessed them, for someone investigating or reading about them, such evidentiality is greatly diminished if not totally lost. Add to this the "implausibility" of such occurrences in terms of scientific and common sense experience, and the hope to convince either the scientific community or the general public of the reality of the paranormal through this type of evidence becomes remote.

Furthermore, if the psi faculty is as widespread as the various surveys taken at different times have suggested—approximately ten per cent of the representative groups polled said that they had had some ostensibly paranormal experience during their lifetime—one would suppose that in the United States alone hundreds of thousands of people each year should experience paranormal phenomena. If they do, why are not the psychical research organizations inundated with such reports which they could then publish in a steady stream to confound all their critics? Henry Sidgwick, the distinguished Cambridge philosopher, who was the principal leader of The Society for Psychical Research from its founding in 1882 for twenty years, pointed out almost ninety years ago that it was incumbent upon the new discipline to discover, investigate, verify, and publish accounts constantly. Why, then, are so few new cases published each year? Why are the same impressive cases cited in book after book as demonstrating some type of phenomenon, and why are these excellent cases mostly very old rather than contemporary? There are several reasons for this most unfortunate state of affairs. First, because, as we have seen, the general climate of opinion regarding the paranormal has remained hostile, people who do experience such phenomena are understandably most reluctant to come forward and report them; when they do, it is frequently many years after the occurrence, documentation is difficult, if not impossible, to obtain or to verify, and they often request anonymity to avoid annoyance and abuse. Second, before publishing any report, researchers must investigate it, gather all the evidence, analyse and weigh it, and prepare a careful, scholarly report. All this takes a great deal of time and would necessitate an enormous staff of trained parapsychologists. Yet, there are very few funds to support such an enterprise. Nevertheless, within the last twenty-five years there have been some collections of such spontaneous cases published in English; for example, both The Society for Psychical Research in Great Britain and The American Society for Psychical Research undertook such surveys, while in recent years Dr. Louisa E. Rhine in the United States and Mr. Andrew Mackenzie in Great Britain have prepared several books reporting such cases. Anyone reading these carefully compiled works will realize that such occurrences do still happen, and that thousands of people have taken the time and trouble to report them and to answer detailed questionnaires and follow-up correspondence. Still, such collections probably represent but a tiny portion of those manifestations of psi that happen daily, become nothing more than a vivid memory and, eventually, an elaborated ancedote as part of a family's lore.

It is because of the inherent difficulties of the spontaneous phenomena carrying conviction to the scientific community that the laboratory approach was initiated and has dominated parapsychology in recent years. Even the experimental data, as already indicated, have produced their own full crop of problems. Assuming that the psi faculty does exist and, under certain conditions, can and will operate, how does one set about determining which facet of the faculty—telepathy, clairvoyance, precognition, or retrocognition—is being used? The answer is very complex and only a brief outline can be given here. In testing for telepathy, the experimenter will lift one card at a time from the pack of twenty-five and look at it while the subject notes his guess as to which of the five designs is printed upon that card. Since the experimenter knows which design is on the card, the subject may obtain the correct design through telepathic reaction with the experimenter. In testing for clairvoyance, the experimenter lifts one card at a time, but does *not* look at it; hence, as he does not know which design is on that card, if the subject guesses correctly, the correct information cannot have come by telepathy, but by the subject's extrasensory perception of the card itself, hence clairvoyantly perceiving the design. Precognition can be tested by asking the subject to guess not the card the experimenter is holding, but the next one; or to ask the subject to guess "down through" the entire deck of twenty-five cards, guessing the order of the designs before they are checked, or guessing the order even before they are shuffled by the experimenter or by a machine.

In fact, however, the process cannot be this simple. Suppose, for example, that the experimenter himself unconsciously and unintentionally perceives the cards in the deck clairvoyantly or precognitively; then, even though he may not look at them, in a test for clairvoyance on the part of the subject, the experimenter unconsciously knows them and the subject may be in telepathic rapport with the experimenter rather than perceiving the cards himself by clairvoyance. Because of this difficulty of separating telepathy, clairvoyance, and precognition, the term "General Extrasensory Perception" or "GESP" was coined to denote a situation wherein there is good evidence for ESP, but one cannot definitively decide which facet of the psi faculty was used.

Eventually, very complicated and circumventing experiments were devised to demonstrate only one of these three facets; randomizing machines and procedures were used to avoid hand shuffling and to minimize the possibility that, by means of PK, the subject was influencing the fall, and hence the order, of the cards. Thus, the techniques of the parapsychological laboratory have become very refined and precise to deal with this most elusive psi; and, as is to be expected in any discipline, there is not complete agreement among researchers as to the facets of psi and their characteristics. One school of thought tends to the view that what has passed for clairvoyance can be adequately explained by telepathy and precognition; another that clairvoyance is the underlying faculty and can account for what has passed as telepathy.

The final large category of mental phenomena consists of the records of mediumistic data. The term "medium" has been used by the spiritualists—a religious group who believe in frequent, if not constant, ability to communicate with the "discarnate" surviving spirits of those who have died—to denote a person who has a highly developed psychic ability. By far the majority of mediums have been women, although some of the very finest have been men. The medium believes that she can, either in a self-induced state of trance, through clairvoyance while awake, or through "automatic writing"—an involuntary writing generally done while in a slightly dissociated state—obtain messages of a "veridical," i. e., verifiable, nature from the discarnate entities which will prove that they survive as self-conscious, remembering, distinctive personalities. In sum, the medium is a go-between, a means of communication between our world and theirs. Psychical researchers often prefer the term "sensitive" or "psychic" because neither of these words implies acceptance of the fact of survival, as "medium" does. In any case, the three terms denote the same type of person.

There are various kinds of sensitives. "Trance mediums" generally go into a self-induced hypnotic state, varying from a very light dissociation to a very deep one; and while in this state, another "personality," termed the medium's "Control," manifests, claiming to be a spirit who will control the medium's body and vocal cords while she is in trance and will "introduce" the spirits who wish to communicate with the "sitter," the person who has arranged the meeting with the medium. Many of these Controls claim to be Red Indians, Orientals, or Negroes, maintaining that the colored races have more highly developed psychic abilities. Sometimes, while in trance, there are striking changes in the medium's voice, facial expressions, vocabulary, and gestures from those when awake. Whether the Control may be, in fact, what he claims, or is merely a secondary personality of the medium, is an issue that has been hotly debated for many years. Word Association Tests given some mediums while awake and their Controls while in trance which showed striking countersimilarities, the use of false names of supposedly deceased persons who were really alive and yet were accepted as spirits by the Controls and other "spirits" are among the items of evidence which point to the secondary personality theory. Yet, there have been some highly trained, experienced, and critical investigators who have maintained that while some Controls may fall into this category, others of truly outstanding mediums seem much more likely to be, in part at least, a discarnate entity. Authorities like Salter and Tyrrell have argued that we must, above all, avoid simplistic concepts of personality construction based upon daily experiences and possibly misleading experimentation in dealing with the complexities of mediumship. Whichever may be the case, that which the sitter seeks and must ultimately judge the medium by is whether he obtains from her veridical information which she could not have obtained normally.

A special category of the trance medium is the "direct voice" medium. This rare type is one who, while in trance, seems to be "taken over" directly by the ostensible communicating spirit, rather than working only through the Control. Some of the most dramatic instances of highly veridical information have occurred with direct voice mediums; and some investigators who have been fortunate enough to sit with a good medium of this nature have written how extraordinarily the voice changed; the idiosyncrasies of the purportedly discarnate entity have sometimes been reproduced with uncanny accuracy, and those present have testified that they felt that another personality, entirely distinct from that of the medium or the Control, was present and had often succeeded in convincing the sitter who should know best that he or she was in fact, and not in pious or desperate hope, the surviving spirit of a loved one. One can well imagine how impressive and moving such an experience would be; yet, as with other spontaneous phenomena, the vicarious impact of the incident upon those who merely read about it is seriously lessened. One's critical faculty rejects such an occurrence as implausible at best, impossible at worst, and says, "I'd have to see it for myself." And this may well be out of the question. Very few have ever had this kind of evidential sitting, although they may have visited many mediums. If such ever did really happen, why cannot it occur regularly? We do not know.

Much more common than the two preceding types is the "clairvoyant" medium, who besides claiming to "see" spirits psychically, often claims "clairaudience," psychic "hearing" of spirit voices and/or "clairsentience," the "sensing" of unseen presences. (It should be noted that trance mediums are generally clairvoyant when awake.) The clairvoyant demonstrates her ability while awake; sometimes she may want to hold an object belonging either to the sitter or to the deceased person the sitter hopes to communicate with: we see again the close connection between clairvoyance and psychometry. Clairvoyants vary enormously in quality. Many give only the vaguest kind of generalities with a string of common first names, frequent illnesses and problems, generalized descriptions of the supposed spirits, etc. Some of these items are bound to apply to almost anyone. Such is hardly convincing evidence of survival. However, there have been, and are today, some clairvoyants who have demonstrated a remarkable ability to furnish very specific and unusual veridical information about the sitter, his family, and some of the deceased relatives or friends he wished to learn about.

Among the most convincing evidence for survival from mediumistic data has been that of a few really fine "automatic writing" mediums. One of these, Mrs. Piper, was possibly investigated more thoroughly over a great many years by trained investigators than any other medium. Often, the trance handwriting has varied sharply from the medium's normal script; it has changed sometimes to approximate that of the purported spirit communicating; the vocabulary, foreign phrases, and eccentricities of expression of the supposed discarnate have, on occasion, been reproduced quite accurately; and highly veridical information has been provided.

The principal question with reference to mediumistic material is: what is the source of any veridical data? Could the medium have obtained the information in some normal way, e.g., through the newspapers, obituaries, subtle enquiries about the sitter's family; through the use of leading questions which cause the sitter to give more information than he realizes about the deceased with whom he wishes to communicate; through shrewd observation of the sitter himself: his clothing, use of language, accent, etc.; through the sitter's unintentionally offering information from which the medium can make logical inferences? Assuming that fraud, inference, and observation can be ruled out for a given item, what could be the source? The most straightforward answer, that of the spiritualists, is that obviously the information comes from the one who claims to furnish it, the surviving spirit of a supposedly dead person, thereby establishing the fact of survival. And this answer has been accepted as valid in some instances by some very distinguished psychical researchers after many years of investigating mediums of all varieties and qualities. But as knowledge about psi has grown, including evidence of its power ranging over human experience with, seemingly, no restraint from either time or space, this simplistic view has been increasingly attacked as inadequately eliminating all possibilities.

Veridical data means data which can be verified. How does one set about verifying an item given by a medium?

One can refer to one's own memory, or to the memory of someone else who should know the facts; one can examine books, other publications, objects, or documents. Therefore, *if* an item is verifiable, some person must be able to prove its accuracy by human knowledge, by some object, or by some document. But if psi is not limited by time or space, if telepathy, clairvoyance, precognition, and retrocognition are at the medium's command unconsciously, it is *possible* theoretically that the medium could telepathically tap the memory of *any* living person, clairvoyantly perceive *any* extant document or object, or precognize *any* future event, and then present this true information to the sitter as coming from a discarnate the convincing personality of which she subconsciously constructs through the use of her intricate dramatic and imaginative mechanism. Such a theory has been termed the "Omnibus," "Extended Telepathy," or "Super ESP" Hypothesis. While there seems little, if any, laboratory data to support the willed use of psi in such a complex manner, this hypothesis does mean that there is a theoretically viable alternative to the surviving spirit as the source of any veridical information. Consequently, it is an ironic twist that as the evidence for the reality of psi has increased, so too have the difficulties of proving conclusively that such a faculty demonstrates a non-physical facet of human personality which could survive physical death.

Suppose that such odd phenomena as we have briefly described, as well as others possibly even stranger, do sometimes happen? Of what possible importance are they, other than to demonstrate that the world gets "curiouser and curiouser"? Besides being vaguely intriguing and faintly amusing anecdotes of absurdly unlikely events, why should anyone take the time to study them seriously? Why have some of the world's greatest scientists, mathematicians, philosophers, and scholars of many diverse disciplines devoted years to their investigation? Because these occurrences and the little-known faculties which underlie them may throw some light upon the most basic queries which every thinking individual must sooner or later pose for himself. Who am I? What does it mean to be a human being? Is man some sort of cosmic jest, chance occurrence, or a carefully wrought creature as part of a larger universal plan? Are time, space, cause, effect, and physicality really the basic characteristics of life and any others wishful imagination? Is the "I-ness" of each person merely a psychological awareness entirely dependent upon the brain, or is it a non-physical faculty which utilizes the brain but which, as the essence of a person, could possibly survive the dissolution of the body and brain at death? Is there any fundamental meaning to human life or is it merely "sound and fury, signifying nothing?"

Psychical research as such does not aim or pretend to answer such questions; its *raison d'être* is the scholarly establishment and analysis of paranormal phenomena which, at the moment at least, do not fit within the known patterns of physical "normality" or scientific explanations currently available. However, insofar as psychical research does demonstrate the existence of such occurrences, and gives evidence that the psi faculty seems independent of known physical, spatial, and temporal limitations, it provides data that bear significantly upon the above questions and any tentative answers one postulates. So it is that those who have studied psychical research thoroughly inevitably turn their attention to the theoretical, philosophical, and possibly religious issues raised by its documented findings.

Surely any field of investigation which can shed light upon the most basic questions a human being can ask must be important, indeed essential, to a thinking person's deliberations; and it is this that has attracted so many of distinguished intellectual gifts and attainments to psychical research. This does not mean, however, that psychical research is an esoteric or elitist field; rather, it is one open to anyone who will take the time to study the findings— spontaneous, experimental, and mediumistic—with an open, critical mind, and decide for himself its significance to him.

The entire purpose of this volume is to assist people to begin and to continue such a study. There is no area which holds such fascinating instances of human testimony, sound and faulty, such an admixture of paranormal and fraudulent phenomena, such possibilities for developing one's critical faculties and broadening one's frame of reference. If, as many of us believe, psychical research is one of the most important disciplines in the world, and if, as is the case, among its students one finds distinguished and sensitive people from around the world, it clearly behooves the thoughtful man to give attention to its records.

No task is more difficult or more worthwhile than the considered attempt to determine the meaning of human existence. The challenge of psychical research is not to be content with the obvious, the commonplace, not to equate physical actuality with ultimate reality, but to delve into all possibilities, however curious they may appear, however disparate from the accepted norm, however obliquely or subtly they may bear upon the search, and to synthesize for oneself a world-view and a philosophy which bring fulfillment. Such a quest may well require of us all that we have and all that we are. No one can expect any more; no one, least of all ourselves, should give any less.

CHAPTER TWO

BIBLIOGRAPHY
FOR THE BEGINNING STUDENT

In this chapter and the next, the student will find annotations for approximately eighty books, organized according to topic, which will be useful in the study of psychical research. They have been carefully selected from a very large number of available volumes but, as with any such personal choice, omission does not, of course, mean that the omitted work is either unsound or worthless. From my experience with lecture and seminar groups, I have found that certain books seem clearer, more interesting, and more helpful than others, and I have based my selection upon those criteria.

I have added, without annotation, other works which I recommend to the student's consideration. The literature in psychical research is enormous, running into thousands of volumes and varying greatly in quality, approach, intent, readability, and importance. Also, many of the types of paranormal phenomena with which psychical research is concerned are integral parts of various esoteric and occult traditions and movements; and while these latter may have considerable value *per se,* their intentions and methodologies are quite distinct and markedly different from those of psychical research. I have not included any works occult in nature, but have limited myself to those which clearly are within the recognized purview of psychical research. I have consulted many acknowledged sources, including bibliographies of research organizations and those in major introductory works, and the student will find, I believe, the most significant contributions to the field covered in either this chapter or the next. I have not, however, except in a few instances, listed any of the vast periodical literature from the *Journals* and *Proceedings* of the principal research bodies.

Because of the great interest in psi phenomena, there has been a constant torrent of popular books on the subject, especially in paperback, during the last several years. Some of these are very sound; many, however, are quite superficial, sensationalistic, overly anecdotal, and often factually wrong. Where I have been able to ascertain that there is a paperback edition of a recommended work, I have indicated this, but there may well be some books so noted that are no longer available in paperback, and, conversely, there may be other books now available in paperback but not so noted.

The distinction between the bibliography in this chapter and that in the next is not hard and fast, but it did seem desirable to indicate to the student that some books would be appreciably more difficult and subtle than others and that certain works presupposed a considerable knowledge of the field in order to be grasped. The division is, however, only a guideline, and each student must decide for himself which works he can by-pass and which are too advanced at the moment.

As with any discipline, the serious student must study the primary sources and assess them critically if he is to understand the material thoroughly. The chief sources in English for such material are the *Journals* and *Proceedings* of the Society for Psychical Research (SPR) and of the American Society for Psychical Research (ASPR), together with the *Journal of Parapsychology*. There are also now defunct publications such as the *International Journal of Parapsychology* which may be of interest to the advanced student. Libraries with sizeable holdings in parapsychological materials will have some, if not all, of these, and the student may learn about availability of both past and current issues of the SPR and the ASPR by writing those organizations, while information about the *Journal of Parapsychology* can be obtained from The Foundation for Research into the Nature of Man. Addresses of these organizations will be found in Chapter Five.

The pamphlet, *Psychical Research, A Selective Guide to Publications in English* (*1959*), available from the SPR, lists many sections of their *Journal and Proceedings* which pertain to specific topics and is a very useful guide to their use. The ASPR also has available a very recent bibliography, R. A. White and L. A. Dale, *Parapsychology in Print* (*1971*), and the Parapsychology Foundation published *A Bibliography of Parapsychology* by George Zorab in 1957 which is worth consulting. Probably the most thorough bibliography on experimental articles is found in Rao's *Experimental Parapsychology,* annotated in the next chapter.

The edition of the work cited either in the annotated section or in the Additional Reading may not be the latest or most easily available, and the student may find that the pagination will vary from edition to edition. Some of the recommended works are currently out of print, but many of the more important books are being reprinted to meet the increased demand, and accessibility of these major treatises is steadily improving.

A.
General Surveys,
Introductions to Psychical Research

Alan Gauld, *The Founders of Psychical Research.* Routledge and Kegan Paul, London, 1968, 387 pages.

> Dr. Gauld, a psychologist, was for some time Editor of the *SPR Journal.* This book recounts the conditions giving rise to the birth of psychical research, the founding of the SPR in 1882, its aims, standards, and problems. There are fascinating biographical portraits of key leaders of early psychical research like Myers, Sidgwick, and Gurney, together with glimpses of other figures who loom large and honorable in the early days: Mrs. Sidgwick, Lodge, William James. The overall view which emerges is of a group of extraordinarily gifted men with a no less remarkable devotion to a search for the truth about contradictory, puzzling, and yet potentially vital phenomena. To understand the care with which psychical research has generally been carried on, one must learn of the tradition; and here Dr. Gauld has traced the genesis of that tradition. In so doing, he has implicitly undermined many of the less valid—and less humane—critics of the discipline. The book is splendidly written.

Rosalind Heywood, *The Sixth Sense.* Chatto and Windus, London, 1959, 224 pages, excellent index. Paperback, Pan

Books, London, 1966. American edition, *Beyond the Reach of Sense*, E. P. Dutton, New York, 1961.

This is a first-rate introduction to psi phenomena and research by one of the leaders of the SPR. Written with a light, deft touch which is charming, there is equally apparent a rigorous balance and a care to assess the various possibilities inherent in any set of data. Mrs. Heywood has a delightful sense of humor, a wide background of general knowledge, and a thorough grasp of the field. The book is greatly enhanced by an Appendix in which some of the major theories of psi in its many facets are summarized and analyzed clearly and cogently.

Raynor C. Johnson, *Psychical Research*. The English Universities Press, Ltd., London, 1955, 176 pages; Philosophical Library, New York, 1956; Funk & Wagnalls, New York, 1968.

Dr. Johnson has produced a clear, readable, and thorough introduction to the field. The explanations are illustrated with some well-chosen examples from the annals of psychical research; the problems inherent in the discipline are discussed; and guidelines as to the evaluation of evidence are given. Johnson also offers some interesting personal theoretical hypotheses which may prick the reader's curiosity to probe deeper. Also, although the book is fifteen years old, there is a sound, if rather brief, bibliography following each chapter. A good index is highly useful.

Charles McCreery, *Science, Philosophy, and ESP*. Foreword by H. H. Price. Faber and Faber, London, 1967, 192 pages, index, glossary. Archon Books, Hamden, Connecticut, 1968, 199 pages.

This is an excellent book dealing with both physical and mental phenomena and offering some original hypotheses and definite suggestions for experimental designs to test them. McCreery, who is a Research Officer at the Institute of Psychophysical Research in Oxford, discusses, with long verbatim extracts, the impressive physical phenomena of Rudi Schneider and Eusapia Palladino, the famous Shackleton experiments of Dr. Soal, and the well-attested case of Larkin and McConnel's apparition. Following this, he adduces hypotheses regarding the characteristics of the state conducive to ESP, the role of EEG evidence regarding the correlation of the alpha rhythm and the ESP state, the influence of drugs, and other variables. His treatment of the knotty problem of repeatability and his suggestions as to its possible solution are important. He writes very clearly.

Gardner Murphy, *Challenge of Psychical Research: A Primer of Parapsychology.* Harper & Brothers, New York, 1961, 297 pages, index; paperback, Harper and Row (Colophon Books), 1970, 303 pages.

A general treatment by one of America's most distinguished psychologists and parapsychologists. Long in the forefront of psychical research, renowned as a scrupulously judicious scholar, Dr. Murphy is in an excellent position to present a balanced view of paranormal phenomena, their investigations and investigators. This volume is remarkable for the lengthy verbatim extracts of actual experimental and investigative articles. Especially noteworthy is the thorough section of key "cross-correspondence" materials. Murphy's careful and clear comments are thought-provoking and will encourage the reader to form his own views and to study further.

Gardner Murphy and Robert Ballou, Editors, *William James on Psychical Research.* Viking Press, New York, 1960; Chatto and Windus, London, 1961, 339 pages, index.

This collection of the writings of Harvard's great pioneer in psychology and pragmatic philosophy is much enhanced by a very perceptive introduction and epilogue by Dr.

Murphy who places James's work and influence within the context of his time. James's determined and courageous insistence that paranormal—or "supernormal" as he called them—phenomena did occur, and must be investigated with the same zeal, impartiality, and care as other ramifications of nature brought his immense prestige to the support of the struggling infant discipline of psychical research. The selections included range from James's important report of the Hodgson control sittings with Mrs. Piper, James's eloquent, yet critical, review of Frederick Myers's work, to his major essay in which he discusses the concept that the brain may be a transmitter rather than, or as well as, a source of consciousness, and his splendid *apologia,* "What Psychical Research Has Accomplished." James had a style that was most precise, yet never dry. This work is essential reading.

J. Gaither Pratt, *Parapsychology, An Insider's View of ESP.* E. P. Dutton, New York, 1966, 300 pages, brief index, brief bibliography.

Dr. Pratt, who has been very active in what he terms the "psi revolution" since 1936, is a highly trained, cautious, and critical parapsychologist who has played a vital role in the development of quantitative experiments and assessment techniques. This book recounts some of the central data for the reality of ESP and PK, discusses some of the principal difficulties in psi research, analyzes various theories, gives a detailed account of the famous Seaford poltergeist case in 1958 which he investigated, provides an especially good treatment of precognition, and includes some sage observations on the significance of the "psi revolution." Pratt writes simply and clearly.

Milan Ryzl, *Parapsychology—A Scientific Approach.* Hawthorn Books, New York, 1970, 216 pages.

This is a broadly popular account written by a Czech

investigator who discovered the impressive subject Pavel Stepanek and who now lives in the United States. In this non-technical introductory work, Ryzl deals with both spontaneous and quantitative work and he gives rather more attention to European parapsychology than most surveys by non-Europeans, which is a welcome feature. There is also a sound summary of Russian research about which the author seems quite well informed. As with any treatment so brief that essays to be an overall view of so vast a field, there are flaws and questionable generalizations; but the book is particularly worthwhile as an easily accessible source of brief information about European work.

Susy Smith, *ESP*. Pyramid Books, New York, 1962, 189 pages.

Despite its rather exotic cover, this paperback provides a basically sound, if superficial, introduction to the discipline. It is neither so scholarly nor so thorough as Raynor Johnson's book, but it is very readable and, in America, probably more easily obtained. Unfortunately, there is neither an index nor bibliography. Miss Smith is a well-known free lance writer about psychical research.

G. N. M. Tyrrell, *The Personality of Man*. Penguin Books, London, 1947, 284 pages, index, bibliography.

One of the most complete and perceptive overall views of psychical research yet published is given by a leading student of the discipline. There are illuminating discussions of qualitative work, experimental efforts by Soal, Rhine, Hettinger, Carington, and others, automatic writing, cross correspondences, mediumship, psychometry, physical phenomena, and an interesting brief chapter on chance. While the treatment of each topic is of necessity rather general and brief, the illustrative instances are carefully selected and his observations are thought-provoking. Tyrrell wrote with great clarity.

B.
Spontaneous Phenomena

Jule Eisenbud, *The World of Ted Serios*. William Morrow & Co., New York, 1967, 357 pages, excellent index, extensive bibliography, 140 illustrations.

The "thoughtography" of Ted Serios has been hailed by some scholars in parapsychology as the most remarkable paranormal phenomenon of our time. In this study of Serios, Dr. Eisenbud, a psychiatrist highly interested for many years in psychical research, explains the sessions in which Serios has produced his extraordinary photographs seemingly by "thinking the picture." In addition, Eisenbud discusses the reasons behind the scientific world's dismissal of paranormal phenomena from a psychiatric point of view which is enlightening. Dr. Eisenbud writes extremely well, with a delightful sense of humor and with an unusual ability to sketch clearly the personality of Ted Serios, his outlook, religious views, psychological make-up, and emotional problems. Altogether, this is a highly readable yet thorough treatment of a fascinating person and his production of remarkable phenomena. The student may wish to pursue his study of Serios's phenomena through the follow-up experiments by Pratt and Stevenson and by Eisenbud given in several issues of the *ASPR Journal* during the last two or three years.

Andrew MacKenzie, *The Unexplained*. Introduction by H. H. Price. Andrew Barker, London, 1966, 176 pages, index. *The Unexplained: Some Strange Cases in Psychical Research*. Abelard-Schuman, New York, 1970, 180 pages.

This collection of about fifteen cases is a very good instance of careful investigation, thorough scrutiny of evidence, and cautious conclusions. Mr. MacKenzie, a professional writer and journalist, is a member of the

Council of the Society for Psychical Research and is a highly competent and respected researcher. Included in his selection is the Seaford poltergeist case, but all the others are British, among them the famous Versailles "adventure" with some new aspects presented, the very puzzling Vandy case, and the important cross-correspondence instance, the "Palm Sunday." This work is one of the few really carefully researched and cogently presented collections of cases in recent years. Mr. MacKenzie writes clearly and holds the reader's interest. There is an admirable brief sketch of the nature and aims of the Society for Psychical Research as an epilogue. This is a fine introduction to the study of spontaneous cases which are the largest and possibly the most interesting segment of the collected data of psychical research.

A. R. G. Owen, *Can We Explain the Poltergeist?* Garrett Publications, New York, 1964, 436 pages, extensive bibliographical notes.

Dr. Owen is a well-known British geneticist and mathematician, for many years a lecturer at Trinity College, Cambridge. Written with the encouragement and support of the Parapsychology Foundation, this is probably the most complete study of poltergeist phenomena in English. Dr. Owen has examined many cases covering virtually every phase of poltergeist activities, has discussed the alternative explanations upon spiritualistic, psychological, fraudulent, hallucinatory, illusory, and paranormal grounds and has presented his own considered—and tentative—opinions. The student will find this engrossing and essential reading, for Dr. Owen has an excellent literary gift and the reader is constantly aware of his erudition and of his judiciousness.

Walter Franklin Prince, *Noted Witnesses of Psychic Occurrences.* Introduction by Gardner Murphy. University Books, New Hyde Park, New York, 1963, 336 pages, index.

This compilation of approximately one hundred and seventy spontaneous cases is divided into categories of professions within which the prominent person who experienced a paranormal occurrence worked and gained his fame, e.g., "Men of Science," "Statesmen," "Theologians," etc. The accounts are generally short and in the original words of the percipient or experient. There is an excellent introduction and explanation by Dr. Prince of the criteria of his choice and of possible conclusions to be drawn. There are also exceedingly thorough indices by nature of phenomena (Apparitions, Premonitions, Raps, etc.) and by percipient. This is an intriguing collection, a good introduction to spontaneous phenomena and to Prince who was possibly America's shrewdest pioneer in psychical research.

Louisa E. Rhine, *ESP in Life and Lab: Tracing Hidden Channels.* Macmillan, New York, 1967, 275 pages.
This is the second of Dr. L. E. Rhine's valuable collections of spontaneous cases taken from over 10,000 which she has gathered over the years. The author analyzes about eighty instances after categorizing them as dreams (realistic or unrealistic), hallucinations, intuitions, or PK cases. Dr. Rhine is known as a "common sense" authority who weighs cases objectively, analyzes them thoroughly, and places them within the context of their specific occurrence as well as within that of their bearing on major issues in psychical research. She also makes it abundantly clear why such anecdotal material often, if not always, unverifiable, is, nevertheless, important. Fascinating reading which raises significant questions about the place of psi within a world system.

Louisa E. Rhine, *Hidden Channels of the Mind.* William Sloane Associates, New York, 1961, 291 pages, brief bibliography.

This book represents the fruit of a ten-year study of Dr. Rhine's large collection of spontaneous cases sent to the Parapsychology Laboratory at Duke University. As her husband, J. B. Rhine, remarks in his Introduction, "The experiences in this book make the data from the laboratory more understandable by demonstrating them, as it were, in action and in life." They may also assist people who have had such experiences to understand what might have occurred. The organization is straightforward and clear. The individual cases are generally presented in the words of the percipients, giving them a lively flavor which exposition would lack. There are perceptive chapters regarding the role of "agent" and "percipient," the problems of time and space, and ostensible discarnate communications. A very fine collection of modern spontaneous phenomena for the student to explore and ponder.

W. H. Salter, *Ghosts and Apparitions.* G. Bell & Sons, London, 1938, 135 pages, glossary.

The author was a prominent figure in the Society for Psychical Research for half a century and knew all the key figures of several generations. A retired barrister, he combined a shrewd judgement of human testimony with great experience in all forms of paranormal phenomena and unusual clarity of expression. This book deals with hauntings, various types of apparitions, and poltergeists, illustrating the different categories of phenomena with about thirty-five instances from the *Journal and Proceedings* of the SPR. Salter examines group perception of apparitions together with the theories advanced to account for it, and in his chapter on poltergeists discusses the role of adolescents, trickery, and other factors, concluding that such phenomena seem rarely, if ever, paranormal. This is a good brief treatment of an important facet of psychical research; but as it was written before Tyrrell's classic

Apparitions, it can fruitfully be compared with that work and with Owens's *Can We Explain the Poltergeist?*

H. F. Saltmarsh, *Foreknowledge.* G. Bell & Sons, London, 1938, 120 pages, glossary.
    The author discusses the evidence for precognition, the theories of Dunne, Price, Broad, Du Prel, and his own "specious present" concept as attempts to account for precognitive occurrences, and the philosophical implications such as free will and determinism. Like Saltmarsh's *Evidence of Personal Survival,* this is clearly written, cogently argued, balanced, and careful. No aspect of psychical research has caused more difficulty in terms of logic than precognition; yet, as Saltmarsh says, it occurs and must be faced. This volume is the best brief introduction to the issue we have, even though it is over thirty years old. Students will find the classification of cases and the criteria used by Saltmarsh illuminating. Comparison with Pratt's discussion of precognition in his *ESP: An Insider's View* would be useful.

Upton Sinclair, *Mental Radio.* Introduction by William McDougall. Revised second printing, Charles C. Thomas, Springfield, Illinois, 1962, 237 pages.
    A major example of qualitative telepathy research, *Mental Radio* was first published in 1930 and was seen then as a very important piece of work, as indicated by the Preface being written by no less a figure than Albert Einstein. But this is no highly technical, dry study; on the contrary, it is lively and most engrossing. The reader should note especially Mrs. Sinclair's description of her state of mind when attempting telepathy or clairvoyance: this is one of the finest explanations we have of the "psychic mood."

Susy Smith, *The Enigma of Out-of-Body Travel.* New

American Library, New York, 1965, 152 pages, index, bibliography.

The style of this, one of several popular accounts of various aspects of psychical research which Miss Smith has produced, is rather informal, and many parapsychologists would not accept all of the evidence adduced as readily as the author appears to do. Nevertheless, this is a good introduction to the kinds of experiences writers mean by "astral travel" or "astral projection," etc., while the bibliography will enable the interested student to read further. The author deals with apparent bilocation, various theories about an "astral," "etheric," "Beta," or "subtle" body, the bearing of out-of-the-body experiences upon survival, whether they are only hallucinatory or objective and veridical in nature, among other topics. She writes clearly and with a sense of humor.

C.
Experimental, Quantitative Studies

J. B. Rhine, *Extrasensory Perception.* Revised edition, Bruce Humphries, Boston, 1964, 240 pages.

Originally published in 1934, Dr. Rhine's first book marked a principal turning point in psychical research, for it provided the first sizeable statistical evidence for psi and led to the laboratory-oriented work which has dominated psychical research since then. Included in this edition is a new chapter sketching the progress during the thirty years between publications. It is an exciting work because it is a pioneer effort, and that sort of commitment, determination to overcome obstacles, and freshness of purpose should enthrall the reader as he learns the astonishing results of those early subjects like Pearce, Linzmayer, Stuart, and others. Essential reading in order to understand modern parapsychology.

J. B. Rhine, *The Reach of the Mind.* Revised edition, Apollo Editions, William Sloane Associates, New York, 1960, 235 pages.

Dr. Rhine's Preface to the revised edition is a useful summary of developments between 1947, when the book first appeared, and 1960. This is a very interesting account of the progress of experimental research which established statistical evidence for the existence of psi, demonstrated that repeatable experiments could be devised and could become increasingly refined and precise. Dr. Rhine postulates some probing ideas about the possible nature of psi based upon the experimental data, and throughout the book demonstrates a remarkably clear and relaxed writing style. An important book which can be usefully compared with Rhine's *Extrasensory Perception* and Soal's work.

Louisa E. Rhine, *Mind Over Matter.* Macmillan, New York, 1970, 390 pages, index, illustrations.

Dr. Rhine presents here the first full discussion of the evidence for PK which has been gathered over a period of thirty-five years both in the United States and elsewhere. She explains the genesis of the research, the first collation after nine years of experimentation, the psychological concomitants of success, various criticisms among parapsychologists and other scientists, discusses possible relationships between ESP and PK, and closes with an outline of the relatively few theoretical frameworks which have been formulated to account for PK. As in her two earlier books, which dealt with spontaneous phenomena, Dr. Rhine has brought together the evidence carefully and she writes simply and clearly. There is, of necessity, a fair amount of statistical material, but its significance is always explained so that the student should have no difficulty in following the argument or understanding the data. The concensus among psychical researchers about PK is not so widespread as that regarding ESP, and the student should be familiar with the evidence so that he can weigh its impact for himself. In no other book has this data been collected and discussed so completely.

S. G. Soal and F. Bateman, *Modern Experiments in Telepathy,* Faber and Faber, London, 1954; Yale University Press, New Haven, 1954, 425 pages, index.

Dr. Soal, for many years a distinguished mathematician at the University of London, is probably the most experienced psychical researcher of quantitative work in Great Britain. Thorough, conscientious, aware of the great need for careful controls, he was fortunate to find two very good subjects who demonstrated remarkable gifts of psi. This book describes his early disappointments in trying to replicate Rhine's work and his later success with Shackleton and Mrs. Stewart. His success in repeating such statistically phenomenal results was of incalculable importance to the progress of psychical research in the laboratory. Both authors write well and explain the conditions and significance of the experiments very clearly.

Robert H. Thouless, *Experimental Psychical Research.* Penguin Books, London, 1963, 148 pages, index, brief bibliography.

Dr. Thouless has been a leader in British psychical research for a good many years. Trained in psychology, he has brought to his work in parapsychology a balanced, open mind together with a freshness and originality of thought which have been very productive. He and Dr. Weisner first suggested the use of the Greek letter "psi" for the psychic faculty, and they have formulated an interesting theoretical framework for psi. In this compact book, Dr. Thouless clearly explains the experimental evidence for psi, how the experiments were conducted, the simple mathematical analysis for extra-chance deviation, the controls needed to obviate criticism, the decline and displacement effects, etc.

He also suggests how "amateurs" can devise their own experiments and how parapsychologists might proceed in new directions to learn more about the operation of psi. His chapter on the issue of critics who accuse experimenters of "cheating" is especially noteworthy. Highly readable.

D.
Philosophical and Religious
Implications of Psychical Research

Raynor C. Johnson, *A Religious Outlook for Modern Man.* McGraw-Hill, New York, 1963, 220 pages, index.

No author has done more to synthesize the data of psychical research with that of science, philosophy, religion, and mysticism into a meaningful pattern than Dr. Johnson. A distinguished physicist by training with an unusual ability to present inherently complex concepts and material in a straightforward, lucid manner, he is judicious, open-minded, and fascinating. He presents what he views as basic questions thinking persons must ask, draws important inferences about possible answers from the human experiences of different kinds of men who have sought spiritual knowledge, and stimulates the reader to challenge his own thinking. This book is an excellent introduction to Johnson's thought as he has crystallized his main theses for the general reader; it is an equally fine way for the student who has gained some knowledge of psychical research and has reflected upon the significance of such data to broaden his framework of thought with a wise and helpful writer.

Raynor C. Johnson, *The Imprisoned Splendor.* Harper & Row, New York, 1953, 424 pages, index, bibliography.

This work has become one of the most widely read syntheses of science, psychical research, philosophy, and religion yet produced. It is the first of Dr. Johnson's works of this kind; the others are annotated in the following chapter. It is not surprising that this book has become so popular because Dr. Johnson has addressed himself to precisely those issues which intrigue all men. He has the advantage of a first-rate mind, thorough scientific training, many years of teaching, broad and deep interests in psychical research and mysticism, and an almost unique ability to pull disparate strands of data and approaches together into a significant whole. Add to this a freedom from dogmatism and a concern for spirituality which is evident throughout. Here is a highly original mind with exciting insights into life's riddles presented in a lucid, and often eloquent, style.

Herbert Thurston, S. J., *The Church and Spiritualism.* Bruce Publishing Co., Milwaukee, 1933, 384 pages.
   The late Father Thurston was certainly one of the most knowledgeable Roman Catholic students of psychical research, spiritualism, and their relation to Christianity. While he naturally supports the Roman Catholic doctrine that attempts to communicate with the dead are wrong, he disagrees with other Roman Catholic writers who hold that all psychic phenomena are fraudulent and argues that, whatever their source or nature, the impressive evidence of men of great eminence and irreproachable integrity substantiates that such paranormal occurrences do happen. Father Thurston had read widely, had witnessed many phenomena, and had already written a good deal about psychic matters before this book was compiled. It is one of the major works by a Roman Catholic expert; and although unfavorable to spiritualism, it is balanced, carefully reasoned, and avoids impugning the good faith of those who view the phenomena differently. Extremely well written.

E.
Mediumship

Hugh Lynn Cayce, *Venture Inward*. Harper & Row, New York, 1964; Paperback Library, New York, 1967, 207 pages, good bibliography of writings about Edgar Cayce, and briefer lists of books about other aspects of the paranormal, dreaming, and meditation.

The literature on Edgar Cayce produced during the last decade is vast, and a movement akin to a cult has developed around his views on reincarnation, diet, geological changes, meditation, etc. All sorts of extravagant claims have been made about Cayce and many of the works concerning his undeniable paranormal gift are quite sensationalistic and unsound. This book by his son is probably the best introduction to Cayce. The author, while believing that his father's teachings are true, does discuss them sensibly and judiciously. He warns readers of the inherent dangers in automatic writing, the planchette, Ouija board dabbling, and psychedelic drugs, while outlining some safer means of expanding one's consciousness. He writes well and gives a good cross section from his father's "readings" to enable the reader to judge the kinds of problems—physical, psychical, and philosophical—with which his father dealt while in trance. It is a pity that Cayce was not thoroughly investigated by trained parapsychologists so that we had completely objective data about his work; but from the stenographic records kept over many years, the evidence of his extraordinary psi faculty seems incontestable. The student can begin a study of this remarkable man through this very interesting work.

Arthur Ford, *Nothing So Strange*. Harper & Row, New York, 1958, 246 pages.

The late Arthur Ford was considered by many to be one of the major sensitives of the last fifty years. He was a gentle, religious man with complex personal problems who was interested primarily in establishing evidence for survival of death and in bringing to bear upon Christian faith the findings of psychical research and the spiritualist movement. This autobiography, written in collaboration with Margueritte Harmon Bro, a well-known religious writer, tells of his family background, of the strange awakening of his psychic gift during the First World War, of the encouragement of Sir Arthur Conan Doyle, of his role in the famous Houdini survival test, his study with the great teacher Yogananda, and his own views on the meaning of life and the impact that conviction of survival can have upon a person's life. Ford was one of the moving spirits behind the formation of Spiritual Frontiers Fellowship. He was neither so introspective nor so intellectual as Eileen Garrett, but his observations about mediumship and its significance are worth considering. The book is most readable.

Eileen J. Garrett, *My Life as a Search For the Meaning of Mediumship.* Rider, London, 1939.

Mrs. Garrett was unquestionably one of the greatest mediums of the century. She was also one of the most intelligent, intellectually curious, and psychologically courageous figures in the history of psychical research. She constantly turned the light of investigators upon her own trance state, trying to understand her unusual gifts, determined to unravel a little the mystery of the human mind and its faculties, and thereby come to some fruitful conclusion about the meaning of life and how her mediumship could help others in such a search. Her motto was really "Know thyself." This book recounts her Irish childhood, religious and personal tensions, personal tragedies, her training as a medium, her emerging psychic sensitivity, and her literary and philosophical influences. Extremely well written.

Gladys Osborne Leonard, *My Life in Two Worlds*. Cassell, London, 1931, 300 pages.

One of the finest of all trance mediums, Mrs. Leonard, during a career of about forty years, cooperated fully with numerous researchers of the Society for Psychical Research and produced some of the most impressive evidence for survival in the annals of psychical research. She and her "Control," "Feda," supposedly an Indian ancestor, gave convincing sittings to hundreds of bereaved people following the fame gained through Sir Oliver Lodge's book *Raymond*. She submitted to various tests, e. g., the book tests and Whately Carington's word association tests, while she was exhaustively investigated over many years by the Rev. Charles Drayton Thomas. Like Mrs. Piper, she was of the utmost integrity, desirous of the fullest cooperation, and there has never been the slightest doubt as to her honesty. In this well-written work, Mrs. Leonard describes how she came to be a medium, various experiences with physical mediumship, the development of her trance work, her own spiritualistic beliefs, and suggestions for psychic development. Whether one accepts all of her personal views, the student will find this book well worth reading for the light it sheds upon the personality and thoughtful conclusions of a very gifted psychic.

Alta Piper, *The Life and Work of Mrs. Piper*. Introduction by Sir Oliver Lodge. Kegan Paul, London, 1929, 204 pages.

Mrs. Piper was undoubtedly the most thoroughly investigated medium of all time. Using both trance and automatic writing, she worked with the leading researchers from 1885 until the end of World War I, and occasionally after that. The controls imposed upon her over eighteen years by Richard Hodgson, Sir Oliver Lodge, William James, and Frederick Myers were exhaustive and constricting, including private detectives, anonymous sitters, forbidding her to read the newspapers, etc. To all of this—

plus the unpleasant physical tests of the depth of her trance like pins, incisions, and sharp chemicals—Mrs. Piper submitted willingly and with enthusiasm, despite the very considerable annoyance and inconvenience to her personal life. All those who worked with her were unanimous in their conviction that she was a lady of indubitable integrity, unquestionable psychic ability, and had produced the most important evidence for survival of any medium. In this book by her daughter, Mrs. Piper's personal characteristics, her home life, as well as her psychic work are described simply and clearly. It is interesting that neither Mrs. Piper nor her daughter state that they are convinced by her own data of the spiritualistic interpretation. This is a sensitive and balanced account with a good sampling of the most important cases of her career by a daughter who often acted as recorder during her mother's sittings, and had a sound critical faculty of her own.

F.
Survival Issue

Paul Beard, *Survival of Death: For and Against.* Hodder & Stoughton, London, 1966, 177 pages, index, brief bibliography.

Although Beard is himself convinced of survival, this is an attempt to weigh some of the principal objections to the survival hypothesis, such as the extended telepathy or Super ESP concept, erroneous claims of ostensible discarnates who turn out to be fictional or still alive, and subconscious imaginings of mediums. The evidence of survival given here consists of generally familiar cases often cited, and there is no reference to American studies of the problem, which is a pity. The book is possibly more important in terms of the conclusions Beard draws as to the *raison d'être* of ostensible discarnate communications, and their bearing upon a person's view of life. He writes very well and perceptively; and one senses that he is a critical sitter, well aware of many crudities in the simplistic spiritualist viewpoint of survival, and eager to present a more reasoned and balanced case for survival.

Hornell Hart, *The Enigma of Survival: The Case For and Against an Afterlife.* Charles C. Thomas, Springfield, Illinois, 1959; Rider, London, 1959.

Hart's book is one of the most important in survival research because it was the first to undertake to examine in an orderly, logical manner both sides of the case, giving fair, accurate representation of the evidence and the difficulties each position entails. Hart was an acknowledged expert in this aspect of psychical research, had established himself as a careful researcher in work at Duke, and played a large part in the census of apparitions in 1956. While he finally plumps for acceptance of survival, his presentation of the contrary case is sound enough that readers may not agree with his conclusion. His "persona theory" to account for mediumistic dramatizations, fictional "spirits," and other such embarrassments of sittings is original and useful. Clearly written in a style that will arrest the attention.

Sir Oliver Lodge, *Raymond.* Methuen, London, 1916, 396 pages, index, illustrations.

One of the most famous of all works on survival, this recounts a series of sittings which Sir Oliver, Lady Lodge, and other members of their family held with Mrs. Leonard and Vout Peters at which they received evidential material purporting to come from the Lodge's youngest son, Raymond, killed in September, 1915. Coming as it did at the height of British losses during World War I and from such a distinguished family, the book was an immediate best seller, going through many printings and editions, and contributing greatly to the growth of interest in psychical research and in spiritualism at that time. Lodge was an experienced researcher, as well as a pre-eminent scientist and educator, and he took precautions to obviate alternative explanations wherever possible to increase the evidentiality; and the book, although fifty-five years old, is still worth reading to see which kind of details can convince some critical, educated people of the identity of a deceased loved one. The last part of the book contains some views by Sir Oliver about life, survival, God, and the significance of life; and they, too, are enlightening as to the philosophical framework not only of Lodge but of many of his contemporaries. Lucidly written by a great scientist who tried to be fair and critical, despite the great emotional involvement he had in the issue, this is an important book to read.

James A. Pike with Diane Kennedy, *The Other Side: An Account of My Experiences With Psychic Phenomena.* Doubleday, Garden City, 1968, 396 pages, excellent bibliography.

This is the account written by the late Bishop Pike of the seemingly paranormal occurrences which followed his son Jim's suicide, and of the Bishop's attempts to learn about paranormal phenomena. In the course of the book there are lengthy sections quoted of records of mediumistic sittings, including the famous television session with the late American medium Arthur Ford. Possibly because of the pressure from the tremendous publicity which attended that television encounter and his desire to present his own, as opposed to the press's, conclusions about his experiences, the book seems to have been written very hastily. It is wordy and awkward in many places, and is not of the same quality of organization and style, with the careful reasoning and prudent presentation of substantiative material, as that of Pike's other works. Then, too, he is dealing with a field in which he was still a neophyte. Nevertheless, it is an interesting account by a controversial, able, and courageous man who tried honestly "to tell it as it is." Useful for the student as an instance of first-hand, subjective material to be contrasted with collected, objective studies as seen in Hart's book.

Kenneth Richmond, *Evidence of Identity.* G. Bell & Sons, London, 1939, 111 pages, glossary.

This is one of the best discussions we have of the problem of identity, the role of the trivial in evidence of identity, the difficulties inherent in the impact of vicarious evidence as opposed to personal experience, the distinction between "conviction" and "proof," demonstrated with clarity of expression which the student will find most helpful. The cases are taken from the SPR's records and have been carefully vetted by Richmond. Many famous instances are included while the student is given annotations as to where he may find the full accounts. Since the issue of identity is at the heart of the survival issue, this volume is an excellent introduction to this thorny problem.

Zoë Richmond, *Evidence of Purpose.* G. Bell & Sons, London, 1938, 112 pages, glossary.

Another volume in the Bell series, although thirty years old, this is an excellent introduction to an important facet of survival research. Mrs. Richmond gives twelve cases of spontaneous apparitions, five of "compulsive impressions," and seven of mediumistic messages, all twenty-four cases having evidence of some purpose behind them, rather than pure randomness or chance coincidence. The cases are well attested, and while not every reader may agree with Mrs. Richmond's assessment of the cause or *modus operandi* resulting in the phenomena, the book is very clearly written, easy to read, with full annotations for those who wish to study the original reports.

H. F. Saltmarsh, *Evidence of Personal Survival From Cross Correspondences*. G. Bell & Sons, London, 1938, 159 pages, glossary, excellent bibliography of cross correspondence materials from the *SPR Proceedings*.

The "cross correspondences" comprise a long series of highly complex automatic writings which many consider the most impressive evidence for survival yet obtained. Saltmarsh was very well versed in the records and had consulted the leading scholars who had explored the intricacies of the puzzles. He has produced an excellent introduction to one of the most important sets of materials in psychical research and has succeeded in demonstrating the complicated designs, subtle allusions to erudite classical motifs, and careful clues which finally led to the solving of some of the problems. He is balanced and considers the various alternative explanations as to the possible sources of the cross correspondences, leaving to the reader his own conclusions as he pursues his studies. Very clearly presented, this is essential reading.

Alson J. Smith, *Immortality: The Scientific Evidence*. New American Library, New York, 1967, 168 pages, index.

Originally published in 1954, this is an attempt by a minister to weigh the evidence which supports the survival hypothesis, the philosophical and religious aspects of the problem, the bearing of precognition and apparent retrocognition upon the issue, what he views as the growing disenchantment with materialism among eminent scientists, and an overall assessment of the impact which parapsychology has had upon modern man's view of himself and his destiny. Smith wrote well, even eloquently, and the student will find this a sound survey of survival evidence and pertinent matters. Some may feel that the author makes generalizations which are dubious and finds more significance in some instances than may be warranted.

While this is not the balanced weighing of pro's and con's one finds in Hart, it is a readable and reasonably thorough account which is easily obtained; as such, it can provide a suitable introduction to the issue.

A.
General Surveys,
Introductions to Psychical Research

Eric J. Dingwall and John Langdon-Davies, *The Unknown—Is It Nearer?* New American Library, New York, 1956.

Martin Ebon, *The Psychic Reader.* World Publishing Co., New York, 1969.

Simeon Edmunds, *Miracles of the Mind: An Introduction to Parapsychology.* Charles Thomas, Springfield, Ill., 1965.

F. S. Edsall, *The World of Psychic Phenomena.* David McKay Co., New York, 1958.

Fabian Gudas, *Extrasensory Perception.* Scribner's, New York, 1961.

C. G. Jung, *Memories, Dreams, Reflections.* Pantheon, New York, 1963.

D. C. Knight, Editor, *The ESP Reader.* Grosset & Dunlap, New York, 1969.

R. Omez, *Psychical Phenomena.* Burns & Oates, London, 1958; Hawthorn Books, New York, 1958.

H. W. Pierce, *Science Looks At ESP.* New American Library, New York, 1970.

J. B. Rhine and J. G. Pratt, *Extrasensory Perception After Sixty Years.* Henry Holt, New York, 1940.

W. H. Salter, *The Society for Psychical Research: An Outline of Its History.* Revised by Renée Haynes, Society for Psychical Research, London, 1970.

Harold Sherman, *How to Make ESP Work for You.* Fawcett, Greenwich, Conn., 1964.

William O. Stevens, *Psychics and Common Sense.* E. P. Dutton, New York, 1953.

B.
Spontaneous Phenomena

J. C. Barker, *Scared to Death: An Examination of Fear, Its Causes and Effects.* Muller, London, 1968; paperback: Dell, New York, 1969.

William Barrett and Theodore Besterman, *The Divining Rod: An Experimental and Psychological Investigation.* University Books, New Hyde Park, N.Y., 1968.

S. Brown, *The Heyday of Spiritualism.* Hawthorn Books, New York, 1970.

Hereward Carrington, *Modern Psychical Phenomena.* Dodd, Mead & Co., New York, 1919.

Robert Crookall, *More Astral Projections.* Aquarian Press, London, 1964.

Robert Crookall, *The Study and Practice of Astral Projection.* Aquarian Press, London, 1961.

Martin Ebon, *Beyond Space and Time: An ESP Casebook.* New American Library, New York, 1967.

Martin Ebon, *Prophecy in Our Time.* World Publishing Co., New York, 1968; paperback: New American Library, New York, 1969.

Martin Ebon, *True Experiences in Telepathy.* New American Library, New York, 1967.

Simeon Edmunds, *Hypnotism and the Supernormal.* Wilshire Books, Hollywood, 1969.

Simeon Edmunds, *"Spirit" Photography*. Society for Psychical Research, London, 1965.

Oliver Fox, *Astral Projection: A Record of Out-of-the-Body Experiences*. University Books, New Hyde Park, N.Y., 1963.

Andrew Lang, *The Book of Dreams and Ghosts*. AMS Press, New York, 1970.

Andrew MacKenzie, *Apparitions and Ghosts: A Modern Study*. Barker, London, 1971.

Andrew MacKenzie, *Frontiers of the Unknown*. Barker, London, 1968; paperback: Popular Library, New York, 1970.

Sylvan Muldoon and Hereward Carrington, *The Phenomena of Astral Projection*. Rider, London, 1951.

Sylvan Muldoon and Hereward Carrington, *The Projection of the Astral Body*. Rider, London, 1956.

Frank Podmore, *From Mesmer to Christian Science: A Short History of Mental Healing*. University Books, New Hyde Park, N.Y., 1965.

L. Rose, *Faith Healing*. Gollancz, London, 1968.

Ronald Rose, *Living Magic*. Rand McNally, New York, 1956; paperback edition: *Primitive Psychic Power*. New American Library, New York, 1968.

Herbert Thurston, S. J., *Ghosts and Poltergeists*. Regnery, Chicago, 1954.

Herbert Thurston, S. J., *The Physical Phenomena of Mysticism*. Burns Oates, London, 1952.

Gordon Turner, *An Outline of Spiritual Healing*. Max Parrish, London, 1963.

Leslie Weatherhead, *Psychology, Religion, and Healing*. Hodder & Stoughton, London, 1951; paperback: revised edition, Abingdon, New York, 1954.

Donald J. West, *Eleven Lourdes Miracles*. Duckworth, London, 1957.

Ambrose Worrall, *Gift of Healing.* Harper & Row, New York, 1965; paperback: *Miracle Healers.* New American Library, New York, 1968.

C.
Experimental, Quantitative Studies

L. W. Allison, *Leonard and Soule Experiments.* Boston Society for Psychic Research, Boston, 1929.

D.
Philosophical and Religious Implications of Psychical Research

Louis K. Anspacher, *Challenge of the Unknown.* Current Books, New York, 1947.

John Langdon-Davies, *Man: The Known and Unknown.* Secker & Warburg, New York, 1960; paperback: *On the Nature of Man.* New American Library, New York, 1961.

Arthur W. Osborn, *The Meaning of Personal Existence.* Theosophical Publishing House, Wheaton, Illinois, 1966.

James A. Pike, *If This Be Heresy.* Harper & Row, New York, 1967.

J. B. Priestley, *Man and Time.* Doubleday, Garden City, 1964; paperback: Dell, New York, 1968.

Alson J. Smith, *Religion and the New Psychology.* Doubleday, Garden City, 1951.

E.
Mediumship

Hereward Carrington, *The Physical Phenomena of Spiritualism: Fraudulent and Genuine.* T. Werner Laurie, London, n.d.

Arthur Ford, *Unknown But Known.* Harper & Row, New York, 1968.

Eileen J. Garrett, *Adventures in the Supernormal.* Creative Age Press, New York, 1948; paperback: Paperback Library, New York, 1968.

Helen Greaves, *The Dissolving Veil.* Churches' Fellowship for Psychical and Spiritual Studies, London, 1967.

Grace Rosher, *Beyond the Horizon.* James Clarke, London, 1961.

E. T. Smith, *Psychic People.* Morrow, New York, 1968; paperback: Bantam Books, New York, 1969.

F.
Survival Issue

A. T. Baird, Editor, *One Hundred Cases for Survival After Death.* Bernard Ackerman, 1944.

Laurence Bendit and Phoebe Payne, *This World and That.* Faber & Faber, London, 1950.

Robert Crookall, *The Supreme Adventure: Analyses of Psychic Communications.* James Clarke, London, 1961.

C. J. Ducasse, *Paranormal Phenomena, Science, and Life After Death.* Parapsychological Monographs No. 8, Parapsychology Foundation, New York, 1969.

Eileen J. Garrett, Editor, *Does Man Survive Death? A Symposium.* Helix Press, New York, 1957.

Arthur Guirdham, *The Cathars and Reincarnation*. Neville Spearman, London, 1970.

S. Ralph Harlow, *A Life After Death*. Doubleday, Garden City, 1961.

J. Head and S. L. Cranston, Editors, *Reincarnation: An East-West Anthology*. Theosophical Publishing House, Wheaton, Ill., 1968.

J. Head and S. L. Cranston, Editors, *Reincarnation in World Thought*. Julian, New York, 1967.

J. B. Hutton, *Healing Hands*. Allen, London, 1966.

James H. Hyslop, *Contact With the Other World*. The Century Co., New York, 1919.

Rosamund Lehmann, *The Swan in The Evening*. Harcourt, Brace & World, New York, 1967.

Sir Oliver Lodge, *Why I Believe in Personal Immortality*. Doubleday, Doran & Co., Garden City, 1929.

Jane Sherwood, *The Country Beyond*. Neville Spearman, London, 1969.

C. Drayton Thomas, *Life Beyond Death With Evidence*. William Collins, London, 1928.

C. Drayton Thomas, *Some New Evidence for Human Survival*. William Collins, London, 1922.

CHAPTER THREE

BIBLIOGRAPHY
FOR THE ADVANCED STUDENT

A.
General Surveys,
Introductions to Psychical Research

C. D. Broad, *Lectures on Psychical Research.* Routledge &
Kegan Paul, London, 1962; Humanities Press, New York,
1962, 450 pages, indices.

This collection of the late Professor Broad's most important lectures covers a wide variety of topics from the
quantitative work of Soal, Rhine, and Tyrrell to
mediumistic studies and the question of survival. Longtime
Professor of Philosophy at Trinity College, Cambridge,
Broad was one of the most eminent academic figures of his
time, a President of the SPR, and a cautious expert in
psychical research. His writing is unusually clear and
compact, and his philosophic erudition evident in the
careful definitions and the logical, balanced consideration

of every alternative explanation. This is one of psychical research's most distinguished books full of profound insights. It is a work to study and to refer to repeatedly.

Whately Carington, *Telepathy: An Outline of Its Facts, Theory, and Implications.* Methuen, London, 1945, 170 pages, good bibliography, index.

Carington had one of the finest minds ever brought to psychical research. His work with qualitative telepathic experiments, mediumistic word association testing, discovery of the displacement effect and its subsequent use to Soal, thoughts on survival—all were important. In this book, he has brought all of his experience, knowledge, and originality of thought to bear upon telepathy in order to construct a theoretical framework to account for its occurrence and thereby, in his view, to answer tentatively at least many of the most perplexing questions posed by paranormal occurrences of various sorts. His Association Theory of "psychons" or clusters of ideas has been fruitful both by its insights and by the criticisms it has encouraged. Carington had a trenchant wit and a wry sense of humor which make this one of the most entertaining books of real consequence in the field. Essential reading for the advanced student.

C. E. M. Hansel, *ESP, A Scientific Evaluation.* Charles Scribner's Sons, New York, 1966, 263 pages, index, bibliography.

Professor Hansel is perhaps the most vociferous antagonist of parapsychology today and this book brings together his strongest criticisms of not only the procedures but the conclusions of parapsychology in their entirety. He argues that since parapsychologists have purported to establish the reality of ESP by so-called "conclusive" experiments which rule out all alternative explanations for the data, these specific experiments must be examined thoroughly and critically to see if this claim is valid. He concludes that it is totally invalid, for in none of these experiments can *only* ESP be the possible explanation; and in many, if not all, the most likely cause for any above-chance results is fraud on the part of the subjects or experimenters or both. He, therefore, finds both Rhine's and Soal's groups guilty of slipshod methods, gross neglect, and spurious results. ESP is not established and all the notions to the contrary are moonshine. This is an important book to read after one is familiar with the field in order to see what some of the principal objections of skeptical scientists are to parapsychology, what light upon improving experiments they can make, and how free of the bias they lay at the door of parapsychologists they themselves are. It would also be useful to read the reviews of this book by Dr. Ian Stevenson in the July, 1967 issue of the *ASPR Journal,* and that by the late R. G. Medhurst in the March, 1968 issue of the *SPR Journal.* Hansel writes clearly and well.

Renée Haynes, *The Hidden Springs: An Enquiry Into Extra-Sensory Perception.* Hollis & Carter, London, 1961; The Devin-Adair Co., New York, 1961, 264 pages, index.
    This is a highly original treatment of psi, considering its manifestations, operation, and significance from various viewpoints: biological, anthropological, sociological, psychological, and religious. Miss Haynes, currently Editor of the *SPR Journal,* is a leader of the SPR, a cautious student of psi, and a devout Roman Catholic. She has discussed the relationship of psi phenomena with basic tenets of Catholicism and finds the relationship largely sympathetic. Her concepts are unusual and cogently argued; but the book requires very careful reading, for her style is recondite, compressed, and full of erudite nuances which the casual reader will miss. The book is difficult to

assess judiciously until one is well-read in psychical research and somewhat cognizant of the ancillary fields she brings to bear upon psi.

Rosalind Heywood, *The Infinite Hive.* Pan Books, London, 1966; U. S. edition: *ESP—A Personal Memoir.* C. P. Dutton, New York, 1963, 252 pages.

Mrs. Heywood is one of Great Britain's most distinguished authorities on psychical research and this is an unusual type of autobiography by a highly gifted woman who is also ʳsychic; she weaves together her personal experiences of a varied kind in many parts of the world, and adds to this pattern her own psychic perceptions together with her intellectual musings upon them and upon the entire range of paranormal phenomena. The work is especially noted for her remarkable balance, her frankness about her own psychic gift, and her intellectual—as opposed to subjective—views about that gift. Exceptionally well written.

Arthur Koestler, *The Roots of Coincidence,* Hutchinson, London, 1972, 142 pages, Postscript by Renée Haynes, bibliography, index.

This work is one of the most impressive syntheses of parapsychology's discoveries and purview with those of physics yet to appear. Mr. Koestler presents in a lucid and captivating fashion the concepts with which the theoretical physicist constantly works and which seem perverse and "impossible" in terms of our ordinary system of sense perception. He discusses Kammerer's "seriality" and Jung's "synchronicity"; proposes his own "holon" schemata to explain the warp and woof of nature, and brings together in an intriguing and persuasive way the various strands of psychical research, mysticism, biology, physics, and philosophy. Essential reading for the advanced student.

F. W. H. Myers, *Human Personality and Its Survival of Bodily Death.* Two volumes. Introduction by Gardner Murphy, Longmans & Green, New York, 1954. Volume I, 660 pages; Volume II, 700 pages, index, glossary.

Myers's book is unquestionably the most famous, most original, and most important single work in psychical research. Some might argue that this should be one of the very first books a student should read, but I have placed it in the second bibliography because I feel that the student will benefit much more from Myers's ideas if he is already well-read in the field. The length alone is daunting, and it is a very complex work, the cap-stone of Myers's research, study, and pondering over several decades. Gardner Murphy's Introduction makes an essential point: it is both foolish and unjust to read Myers's theories without constant referrals to his substantiating material in the Appendices. Myers's death left the work unfinished, and it was collated into its final form by co-workers at the SPR. It is truly a monumental synthesis of analytical data from the new psychology and psychiatry, physiology, philosophy, and, of course, psychical research. Here one finds for the first time the concept of the "subliminal self" as Myers termed it, together with a theoretical framework for exploring its operation and its bearing upon paranormal phenomena. The entire question of the body-mind relationship, the issue of what constitutes a personality—such central matters are at the core of psychical research and their serious consideration begins with this most remarkable book.

F. W. H. Myers, *Human Personality and Its Survival of Bodily Death.* Foreword by Aldous Huxley. One volume, abridged by Susy Smith. University Books, New Hyde Park, New York, 1961, 416 pages, Index.

For this one volume version of Myers's classic, Miss Smith has culled out much of the substantiating material from the large Appendices, and has placed what she considers the most important of the supportive data within the text itself, so that the book is much more easily handled and read. The central theories are, of course, retained, and there is sufficient corroborative material left to show that Myers had a sound basis for a given point. For some, this presentation may be the best introduction to Myers, leaving the original, full work for a later stage of study. Any abridgement, especially by more than half, changes the impact of a work; but Miss Smith has been judicious in her retentions, and the reader can certainly follow Myers's thought and appreciate the range of his mind. Myers, of course, would be the last to insist that what he wrote at the turn of the century would be equally valid today, as knowledge in psychical research and psychology has greatly advanced; and the issue of survival has proven a much more difficult and complex one than he envisaged. Whatever its drawbacks, however, this is the most essential single work the student can read.

Eugene Osty, *Supernormal Faculties in Man.* Methuen & Co., London, 1923, 242 pages, index, numerous bibliographical references in the notes.

Osty was a leading French researcher who directed the Institut Métapsychique International in Paris for a number of years, collaborated with many prominent investigators, and wrote widely upon psychical research. In the course of this volume, he examines the mechanism of sensitives, or "metagnomes" as frequently termed by European students in the 1920's and 30's, and postulates various theories as to the psychological makeup, processes, and affective factors in the paranormal information produced. Osty was a physician and very interested in the physiological as well as psychological aspects of the subject. There is a wealth of data, hundreds of instances drawn principally from his own experiences, and many references to other European, especially French, work which will be of great value to the student. The style is rather turgid and repetitive, for Osty was trying for clarity and precision; but it will repay study.

Charles Richet, *Thirty Years of Psychical Research.* W. Collins Sons & Co., London, 1923, 626 pages, index.

Richet, winner of a Nobel Prize, was one of the leading physiologists of his day, and although at first rejecting the reality of paranormal phenomena in the 1870's, he came to accept both mental and physical phenomena of various types. He coined the term "ectoplasm" for the quasi-physical substance ostensibly extruded from physical mediums; he investigated many of the most prominent mediums, especially Eusapia Palladino and Eva C., and he was adamant that all such phenomena must meet scientific standards while avoiding all trappings of occultism, spiritualism, and religious overtones. This is a major work by one of the great scientists of France, and it is in sharp contrast to the writings of nearly all British and American psychical researchers who have felt that the evidence for physical phenomena, especially ectoplasmic materializations, falls far short of that needed for acceptance. While he examines all types of phenomena, the bulk of the book deals with the four kinds he is convinced of: "cryptaesthesia," his term for General Extrasensory Perception, "telekinesis," or psychokinesis, precognition, and ectoplasmic manifestations. His firm rejection of the survivalist hypothesis, despite his conviction of the paranormal phenomena, was unusual among his generation. He was a man of vast erudition, a wry sense of humor, and a Gallic lucidity of style. No student can afford to ignore this summary of Richet's decades of painstaking experimentation, keen observation, and courageous stand in defiance of his orthodox scientific brethren.

Gertrude Schmeidler, Editor, *Extrasensory Perception.* Atherton Press, New York, 1969, 166 pages.

Dr. Schmeidler is one of the leading American parapsychologists, and in this volume she has collected nine papers—all previously published—and has made perceptive comments about each, as well as providing an overall context for them with an excellent introductory essay. The papers include Hansel's attack on the Pearce-Pratt series, the rejoinders of Pratt and Rhine, the Anderson-White study on the bearing the relationship between students and teachers had on clairvoyance tests, and interesting aspects of ESP stimulation—social and personal predilections—different variance factors in ESP phenomena and assessments, and dream studies. The selection is overall of a high quality and is representative of the really sound research being carried on in the discipline. As such, it presents the advanced student with a fine opportunity for conveniently studying current research.

J. R. Smythies, Editor, *Science and ESP.* Routledge and Kegan Paul, London, 1967; Humanities Press, New York, 1967, 306 pages.

This volume consists of thirteen essays by distinguished scholars from the disciplines of psychiatry, philosophy, physics, anthropology, biology, and psychology, as well as psychical research. Among the contributors are such well-known figures as Sir Cyril Burt, C. D. Broad, Sir Alister Hardy, Rosalind Heywood, Francis Huxley, H. H. Price, and Emilio Servadio. The papers are of varying quality and pertinence, but the student will find it worthwhile to compare the different attempts to account for ESP in terms of the writer's own discipline with some interdisciplinary viewpoints. C. D. Broad's essay stands out for its usual lucidity and severity of logic while Burt's lengthy essay is brilliant. The Appendix by Dr. Beloff on "A Guide to the

Experimental Evidence for ESP" is a very useful item for the student and the general reader.

René Sudre, *Parapsychology.* Citadel Press, New York, 1960, 401 pages, index, numerous bibliographical references in notes.

Sudre in his youth knew the principal French researchers such as Geley, Richet, and Osty, and is in the tradition of these figures in being strongly anti-spiritualistic, highly critical of the British and American investigators for ignoring or rejecting what he feels is indisputable evidence for the reality of physical or "teleplastic" phenomena, while constructing needless and complex theories of hallucination to avoid the objective nature of such occurrences. Furthermore, he resolutely deprecates the great emphasis upon the quantitative approach: "Decimals have never convinced anyone." Sudre gives a very interesting account of the historical development of research into the paranormal, with special attention to the European work. The student will find his style clear, if often acerbic toward those with whom he disagrees (and they seem legion). At a time when physical phenomena (with the exception of some PK experiments) seem virtually non-existent in the English literature, it is certainly worthwhile to study a very different viewpoint.

G. N. M. Tyrrell, *The Nature of Human Personality.* George Allen and Unwin, London, 1954, 120 pages, index.

The last of Tyrrell's books, this represents the author's most mature reflections about the overall significance of psychical research, man's innate faculties, his difficulties in overcoming his evolutionized common sense outlook to recognize the reality of psychic phenomena, the bearing of paranormal occurrences upon religion, and other philosophical and psychological discussions. It would be helpful to have read Tyrrell's *The Personality of Man* before undertaking this book, since it is, in a sense, a sequel to the earlier work; but it can perfectly well be read on its own. As in all of Tyrrell's writings, his style is lucid, his arguments cogent, his erudition deep and wide, covering not only psychical research but many ancillary fields as well.

G. N. M. Tyrrell, *Science and Psychical Phenomena* and *Apparitions.* University Books, New Hyde Park, New York, 1961, with a Foreword by Laura A. Dale to *Science and Psychical Phenomena,* and a Preface by Professor H. H. Price to *Apparitions, Science,* 371 pages, index, *Apparitions,* 168 pages, appendix of cases.

Science and Psychical Research was first published in 1938, as a general treatment of the entire discipline. As such, it was one of the earliest in English and remains one of the best. By the time he wrote the book, Tyrrell had thirty years of experience in psychical research and over fifteen of full time work at it; he was a highly trained engineer, fully versed in the quantitative approach, an acute student of the qualitative aspect, and a widely read and original thinker. Add to this his excellence of style, balanced viewpoint, and sense of humor and the student will find that thirty-five years after it was written, this is a splendid overall view of the field, which will pique him to study further and to think for himself about the underlying significance of the whole.

Apparitions is generally conceded to be the most original work yet produced about this phenomenon and the greatest single contribution to psychical research of Tyrrell. Professor Price's Preface gives a clear and useful summary of Tyrrell's thesis so that the student can have the general framework in mind before studying the author's theories. Like all of Tyrrell's work, this is carefully thought out, painstakingly substantiated, and lucidly presented. Essential for every student of psychical research, after he has a sound understanding of the basic data.

L. L. Vasiliev, *Mysterious Phenomena of the Human Psyche.* University Books, New Hyde Park, New York, 1965, 204 pages, illustrations, index.

Vasiliev was a highly regarded Russian physiologist before he became involved in the first parapsychological research at Leningrad University, and his work aroused both interest and controversy on both sides of the Iron Curtain. He examines the evidence for psychokinesis, telepathy, clairvoyance, the role of sleep and dreams in possible paranormal phenomena, the use of psychedelic drugs in such experimentation, and theories about the nature of extrasensory perception. Naturally, he rejects any dualistic, much less any spiritualistic, explanations about survival or mediumship; instead, he discusses a new Russian science, "thanatology"—the study of the nature of death. He seems to have felt that in ESP some form of energy from the brain was utilized and that it was essential to discover this energy so as to confute the occult, mystical, and other superstitious leanings which "pollute" western parapsychology on occasion. This is an important book for an understanding of Russian research and the current interest in their work.

D. J. West, *Psychical Research Today.* Penguin Books, London, 1962, 224 pages, index, bibliography in references, eight photographs.

This is a highly skeptical account by a former Research Officer of the SPR and a trained psychiatrist. West considers that the evidence for paranormal faculties among mediums, physical phenomena, apparitions, haunts, poltergeists, spiritual healing, etc., is so scanty and so plagued with fraud and credulity as to warrant little acceptance. There is, however, he holds, enough evidence for the presence of ESP from the laboratory experiments, even though confirmation by frequent replication has not been so far possible. He suggests various new attacks, discusses some of the more important exploratory theoretical views, and urges more experiments by trained researchers. West is one of the most cautious and critical of all writers on psi phenomena, and it is useful to compare his explanations as a psychiatrist who accepts the existence of ESP with those of Hansel as a psychologist who rejects ESP. The book is clearly written.

B.
Spontaneous Phenomena

Everard Feilding, W. W. Baggally, and Hereward Carrington, *Sittings With Eusapia Palladino and Other Studies.* Introduction by E. J. Dingwall. University Books, New Hyde Park, New York, 1963, 324 pages.

This very important volume contains the full account of about fifteen sittings undertaken with the famous—or infamous, depending on one's point of view—Italian physical medium Eusapia Palladino, together with several other significant reports on other mediums and physical phenomena. Everard Feilding was an extraordinarily acute and experienced investigator, while Hereward Carrington was an expert on physical phenomena and an excellent amateur magician, and W. W. Baggally cooperated in many investigations for the SPR. Probably no other physical medium, except "Margery," has aroused such controversy as Palladino, an earthy, erotic Italian who cheated whenever she could, and yet seemed on occasion to produce most remarkable phenomena under stringently controlled conditions. The student will benefit from Dr. Dingwall's notes and comments, for he is noted as one of the most knowledgeable and critical investigators in the field. The complexity of psi and the difficulties and perseverence required of the dedicated psychical researcher are nowhere more vividly presented than in the studies contained in this book.

Edmund Gurney, Frederick W. H. Myers, and Frank Podmore, *Phantasms of the Living.* Trubner & Co., London, 1886; abridged edition prepared by Mrs. Henry Sidgwick, Kegan Paul, London, 1918; E. P. Dutton, New York, 1918, *Phantasms of the Living* and *On Hindrances and Complications in Telepathic Communication,* abridged and edited by Eleanor Sidgwick, University Books, New Hyde Park, New York, 1962. The edition annotated is the 1918 version. lx plus 520 pages, table of cases, lengthy synopsis of each sub-heading in each chapter.

The original version of this classic work, in 1886, was in two enormous volumes, containing over seven hundred cases with discussion and theoretical postulations. The abridged version has retained slightly less than two hundred of these, omitting all but first-hand accounts. Thus, as Mrs. Sidgwick notes in the Preface, the cases retained must be taken "as typical cases, not as exhibiting the mass of evidence obtainable at the time." More than enough remains, both of cases and of the original discussion, to indicate the strong case for telepathy which Myers and Gurney made, and to show the brilliance of these two early experts in psychical research. The rolling majesty of their writing is arresting, if foreign to the clipped style of today. In recent years, there has been a tendency in some quarters to make light of the work of the early researchers, a suggestion that they were less than critical and too much concerned with possible religious overtones of paranormal phenomena. From a close reading of this book—together with Myers's classic *Human Personality* and early volumes of the *SPR Proceedings*—the student will find that such modern strictures are largely invalid. In Myers's eloquent Introduction to this book, for example, he is most cautious about the bearing upon the survival issue of the infant psychical research discipline. More years of research convinced him of survival, but it is a capital error to suppose that he, or his distinguished colleagues, desperately twisted the data to fit their own philosophical predilections or religious yearnings. This monumental study is essential for the advanced student; here one can find the seedtime for those canons of evidence and strict standards of scholarship which only the critics of psychical research ignore.

Walter Franklin Prince, *The Case of Patience Worth.* University Books, New Hyde Park, New York, 1964, 509 pages.

No single case has been more carefully and thoroughly investigated, analyzed, and presented than that of Mrs. Curran, a middle-class St. Louis housewife who, beginning in 1913, with a Ouija board, produced remarkable literary works: poems, novels, epigrams, which displayed not only unusual creative power and originality, but unparalleled spontaneity of production. The ostensible source was the spirit of "Patience Worth" who claimed to have lived in the seventeenth century. Dr. Prince spent ten months investigating Mrs. Curran, her family, education, friends, and literary abilities and presents this painstaking research in one of the classic books of psychical research. As puzzling today as when it was exhaustively examined in 1927, the case poses important questions, as yet unanswered, about the nature and extent of the subconscious, innate histrionic abilities, and the range of imagination and subliminal information-gathering which must be postulated to vitiate the spiritist hypothesis. Essential reading.

Stewart Wavell, Audrey Butt, and Nine Epton, *Trances.* E. P. Dutton and Co., New York, 1967, 253 pages, twenty-four illustrations, bibliography, index.

Far too little work has been done among primitive

peoples and their beliefs and practices which are ostensibly paranormal in nature. This book by Butt, an Oxford anthropologist, Wavell, an explorer who has lived much of his life in the Orient, and Epton, a travel writer who has had many experiences with such cultures, is, therefore, very welcome. The trio of authors apparently came together as a consequence of a BBC broadcast, and while the book is not a scholarly anthropological study, it is a sound work, exceedingly well written, with much of interest to the student of psi. Butt has studied the Akawaio Indians in the Amazon jungles for some years and the chapters on the "shamans" are intriguing. Other groups dealt with include the Gnaoua of Morocco, the Temers of Malaya, the Bali Barong performances with deadly "kris" daggers, various mystical groups of Algeria, Sumatra tribes, etc. Since we know so little about mediumistic trance, the interesting features which seem common among such divergent cultures in the inducement of trance are significant to psychical research. Healing and communication with spirits are important functions of the trance state among the peoples studied here, and the student will find much of importance in this book, not least the useful bibliography to anthropological studies.

C.
Experimental, Quantitative Studies

Haakon Forwald, *Mind, Matter and Gravitation: A Theoretical and Experiential Study.* Parapsychological Monographs No. 11, Parapsychology Foundation, New York, 1970, 72 pages.
 Mr. Forwald has written a fine summary of twenty years of research into PK effects with dice of varying size and weight. A very able and careful Swedish electrical engineer, Forwald has written several articles for the *Journal of*

Parapsychology about his findings and computations regarding the physical aspects of PK, but this pamphlet is an easy way for the student to learn about his research and his theoretical explanations. There have been several criticisms directed at Forwald by parapsychologists: first, that most of his work has been done alone, while he acted as both subject and investigator, so that there is no witnessed substantiation for many of his results (some, however, were gained at Rhine's laboratory); secondly, that his predilection for a gravitational explanation due to his professional training may have led him to ignore or seriously to underestimate the psychological causative factors in PK. Nevertheless, this small but important monograph is a key work in the growing literature about PK.

K. Ramakrishna Rao, *Experimental Parapsychology: A Review and Interpretation.* Charles C. Thomas, Springfield, Illinois, 1966, 255 pages, index, glossary, exhaustive bibliography of over 1200 items, mostly articles pertaining to experimental work.

Rao has set out to summarize the experimental development of parapsychology since Rhine wrote his book *Psychical Research After Sixty Years,* in 1940. Much of great importance has occurred in that quarter of a century and, Rao, for some years associated with Rhine at Duke University and now pursuing research at an Indian university, is an experienced researcher. His interest lies almost solely with laboratory, quantitative work, as he feels that only in such data can "proof" of the psi faculty be attained. Included in this work are accounts of all significant experiments during a twenty-five year period, plus a critical examination of various theories of psi by Rhine, Roll, Murphy, Broad, Flew, Price, Carington, Tyrrell, and others. Rao's style is rather academic and sometimes even ponderous; but he has a keen mind, ideas of his own, and uncompromising evidential standards of a quantitative nature.

J. B. Rhine and J. G. Pratt, *Parapsychology: Frontier Science of the Mind.* Charles C. Thomas, Springfield, Illinois, revised edition, 1962, 224 pages, bibliography, index.

Intended as "A survey of the field, the methods, and the results of ESP and PK research," this volume, co-authored by two of the most experienced and respected parapsychologists, is a straightforward, carefully written account, emphasizing the objective, experimental work performed over the last forty years. There are an excellent glossary and long bibliographies both to books and articles covering the entire range of paranormal phenomena, data, and theories. This work is recommended following some familiarity with the experimental material of psychical research. It is very readable.

Gertrude R. Schmeidler and R. A. McConnell, *ESP and Personality Patterns.* Yale University Press, New Haven, 1958, 110 pages, appendices, bibliographical references, index. Preface by Gardner Murphy.

Dr. Schmeidler is best known for her "sheep" and "goat" experiments, and they are the major basis for this book, the statistical work for which was done by Dr. McConnell. a biophysicist as well as an experienced parapsychologist The authors have aimed at satisfying the professional scientist without bewildering the interested layman, and have succeeded admirably. The statistical tables are clear, the statistical terminology is remarkably well explained, and sections of a very technical nature can easily be skipped. The material dealing with the ESP subjects' response to Rorschach and other psychological testing, the experimentation with concussion patients, and the discussion of new areas of research needing attack are fascinating. Both write extremely well; this is scholarly parapsychology at its best and most readable.

Charles T. Tart, Editor, *Altered States of Consciousness: A Book of Readings.* Wiley, New York, 1969, 575 pages.

This is the best introduction to this important topic yet published. While the work is not directed at the layman, the writing is generally so clear that the advanced student should not find undue difficulty with the material, especially as it has been subdivided into useful sections dealing with hypnosis, psychedelic drugs, meditation, the "hypnagogic state" between sleeping and waking, dreams, etc. There are experimental and theoretical discussions of the various states which may shed a good deal of light upon the workings of the psi faculty. There is a massive bibliographical reference section which the student wishing to explore further will find invaluable, although much more has been published since this volume was prepared. While only two of the papers are directly concerned with psi phenomena, there seems a growing interest among parapsychologists about altered states of consciousness as they may bear upon conditions favorable to psi, and the advanced student should be aware of this aspect of work.

René Warcollier, *Experimental Telepathy.* Boston Society for Psychic Research, Inc., Boston, 1938, edited and abridged by Gardner Murphy, 294 pages, glossary.

A most useful collection of sixteen papers by a thoughtful, thorough, and imaginative French researcher, this volume contains a mine of speculative concepts as well as valuable experimental work illustrated by many drawings of the telepathic targets and attempts. Warcollier was a chemical engineer who brought to psychical research a sound scientific background, rigid standards of work, and a fertile mind. The student will find his ideas refreshing and germinal, his stance open minded and frank. Although some of the articles are fifty years old, they remain well worth studying both for the quality of the experimental work in telepathy they represent and for the shrewd observations about the problems of experimentation in telepathy and other paranormal fields.

D.
Philosophical and Religious Implications

Raynor C. Johnson, *The Light and the Gate.* Hodder and Stoughton, London, 1964, 312 pages, index.

Dr. Johnson writes about four men who have greatly influenced his thinking about the meaning of life: the Irish poet and mystic A. E. (George Russel), the Australian novelist and diplomat, Ambrose Pratt, the American-born Buddhist sage, Venerable Sumangalo, and the British preacher and writer, Dr. Leslie Weatherhead. Included are four essays which connect each figure's principal concerns. As with all of Johnson's works, this is mind-stretching, superbly written, and challenging. For the student who has reached that point where he ponders the significance of the expanded world view which psi phenomena present, this book will suggest new vistas; for each of these men is remarkable in his own way, and each has sought to find "the light and the gate" in his own manner.

Raynor C. Johnson, *Nurslings of Immortality.* Hodder and Stoughton, London, 1957, Harper and Bros., New York, 1957, 279 pages, index.

In this, his second synthesis of philosophical, religious, mystical, scientific, and parapsychological data, Johnson presents the case for Douglas Fawcett's philosophy of Imaginism, and discusses how well it seems to answer the riddles of man's existence, God's nature, purpose in human life, the existence of evil, etc. Because Fawcett's basic concept is quite different from our normal philosophical frame of reference, parts of the work are quite difficult to grasp, depite Dr. Johnson's usual lucid style and careful analogies. It gives the thoughtful reader much to ponder; but it would be helpful to have read Johnson's *The Imprisoned Splendour* and *A Religious Outlook for Modern Man* first, and to have a firm grasp of psychical research before undertaking this work.

A. G. N. Flew, *A New Approach to Psychical Research.* Watts, London, 1953, 158 pages, index, bibliography, two appendices.

Professor Flew is a highly skeptical student of psychical research who is principally concerned with the problems of language, precision in concepts, philosophical issues, and the nature of requisite evidence to establish the reality of psi phenomena. He argues that the qualitative evidence is so dubious because of the notorious inaccuracy of human testimony that it can be given little credence. We are left, therefore, with the statistical evidence, which is also suspect in some respects because of loose experimentation controls. He, however, feels that there is sufficient basis for the hypothesis of psi on statistical grounds, but rejects utterly the philosophical implications of mind-body, religious and survivalist overtones, and what he deems are wildly improbable and unwarranted assumptions about the undermining of physicalistic or materialistic views of man's nature by the psi evidence. This is a very stimulating book by a professional philosopher who has read the evidence, has a keen mind, an incisive and amusing style, and original ideas. His approach is similar to D. J. West's, but with a philosophical rather than a psychological bent. An important book to read and compare with critical works like Hansel's, Lamont's, and Rinn's.

Sir Alister Hardy, *The Divine Flame.* Collins, London, 1966, 254 pages.

This is the second series of Gifford Lectures at the University of Aberdeen, and in this volume, Sir Alister is concerned less with biology and evolution than with psychology, anthropology, parapsychology, and theology. Because he is dealing with issues not so directly within the purview of his own scholarly expertise, these lectures, while preserving the same splendid quality of writing, are upon possibly less sure ground; or at least open to a wider variety of interpretation and criticism. The central points the author makes are that the evidence of physical science does not contravene the possibility of a divine order or divine being, as materialists have argued; that psychological, especially Freudian, interpretations of myths and primitive magical rites may well be only partial explanations; that the testimony of outstanding mystics as well as ordinary people bear evidence to the divine reality; that psychical research has suggested, if not definitely demonstrated, that a dualistic view of man is highly plausible, i.e., that brain and mind may well be distinct; and that, consequently, the fashionable view that the concept of a God is merely an exteriorized psychological construct to meet deep-seated human needs is not necessarily valid. There is strong empirical evidence to merit the belief in a "divine flame" pervading the universe, open to the questing human being, and giving to existence meaning and dignity. Like the first volume, this is exciting and inspiring reading.

Sir Alister Hardy, *The Living Stream: A Restatement of Evolution Theory and Its Relation to The Spirit of Man.* Collins, London, 1965, 292 pages.

This collection of the first series of the Gifford Lectures at the University of Aberdeen is an important synthesis of the author's ideas. One of Great Britain's most distinguished zoologists, a former President of the Society for Psychical

Research and thus a highly qualified expert in psychical research, Hardy combines his knowledge of biology and parapsychology with his philosophical and religious thoughts. His treatment of the evolutionary theory as it has developed since Darwin is fascinating, for he writes superbly, and as the lectures were given for a non-specialist audience, he has aimed at the layman in his account. Hardy believes that the evolutionary schemata is far less deterministic in an environmental sense than has been generally understood, and postulates an idea of "organic selection" through which species engage in environmental selection and develop organic changes to meet the needs of the new environment. But it is in the final lectures that the relation of the work with psychical research is most apparent. Hardy argues that psychical research bears upon the materialist dominance in thought about human personality and demonstrates that this viewpoint is not so impressive as many think. Rather, he holds that telepathy demonstrates that mind is something else or more than brain and possibly more than individual mind; if so, he feels that this might explain some of the problems of evolutionary development. Finally, in his lecture on "Natural Theology in the Evolutionary Scheme," Sir Alister eloquently presents his belief in a pervasive force—a Divine Power—which while not synonymous with the traditional personalized God, is nevertheless within extrasensory reach by prayer. There are few scientists who combine the knowledge of their own specialty with that of psychical research and possess such a deft literary ability as Sir Alister. This book is an exciting excursion with a wise and thoughtful scholar.

Lawrence LeShan, *Toward A General Theory of the Paranormal: A Report of Work in Progress.* Parapsychology Foundation, Inc., New York, 1969, 112 pages, index.

This brief, very clear monograph is one of the most

important theoretical works to appear in parapsychology for some time. Dr. LeShan has presented a hypothesis that each individual has his own reality within which he operates and that there are various types of Individual Realities or IR's: common sense, scientific, mystical, and clairvoyant. He discusses how congruent the theoretical-scientific, the S-IR, and the mystic-clairvoyant, the C-IR, have become with the new physics and quantum theory, and how incongruent these are with the common sense IR. He examines the hypothesis through the experiences of mystics and sensitives, especially Mrs. Eileen Garrett, and through the writings of scientific theorists like Planck, Heisenberg, and Eddington. It is a fascinating and encouraging small book which requires careful study, based on a very thorough knowledge of both the data and theories of psychical research. Essential reading for the advanced student.

G. N. M. Tyrrell, *Grades of Significance.* Rider, London, Second Edition, 1947, 221 pages.

First written in 1930, Tyrrell in his Preface to the Second Edition, terms the essay "not an attempt to condense a system of philosophy, but only a parable intended to encourage a peculiar orientation of thought in the reader's mind." This orientation is found in his concept of "aspects" of reality and the varying significance to be attached to them depending upon one's presuppositions, personality stance, and level of spiritual awareness. The discussion of psychical research, its connections with spiritualism, religion, scientific materialism and determinism, and Tyrrell's illuminating comments on mysticism are all most stimulating and thought-provoking. A germinal work, not only for Tyrrell himself, but for any student of the paranormal.

E.
Mediumship

Eileen J. Garrett, *Many Voices: The Autobiography of A Medium.* G. P. Putnam's Sons, New York, 1968, 242 pages, index.

This is the last of Mrs. Garrett's books to be published, and while there is of necessity some repetition of experiences to be found in her *Adventures in The Supernormal* and *My Life As A Search for the Meaning of Mediumship,* in *Many Voices* she has presented her most mature and considered views upon matters psychic. She was acknowledged as one of the greatest of all mediums, quick-witted, a shrewd businesswoman and administrator, with Celtic wit and charm. During her long life she came into contact with a host of remarkable people and her reminiscences bristle with literary figures like Joyce, Hardy, A. E., and Conan Doyle, as well as noted psychical researchers. Her chief monument is the Parapsychology Foundation which has generously supported psychical research for many years, and she recounts its inception and aims. Ever seeking, always questioning, probing, never satisfied with the facile or simplistic answer, this book shows the thoughts and experiences of one of the most remarkable women of our time.

Geraldine Cummins, *Swan on a Black Sea: A Study in Automatic Writing: The Cummins-Willett Scripts.* Introduction by C. D. Broad, autobiographical note by Geraldine Cummins. Samuel Weiser Inc., N.Y., 1970, 168 pages.

This is a compilation of scripts automatically written by the well-known Irish sensitive, Geraldine Cummins, and purporting to be dictated by the late Mrs. Coombe-Tennat who, under the pseudonym of Mrs. Willett, played a key role in the famous "cross correspondences" in the first two decades of this century. Not until after her death in 1956, was it publicly known that she was "Mrs. Willett." The value and quality of these scripts has been assessed quite differently by various parapsychologists, but they are clearly the most important mediumistic materials to be published for quite some time; and whatever their true origin, they reveal the extraordinary sense of personality, identity, and the highly veridical information which such materials, at their very rare best, can present. Professor Broad's Introduction is most perceptive and valuable. Essential reading.

Susy Smith, *The Mediumship of Mrs. Leonard.* University Books, New Hyde Park, New York, 1964, 260 pages, bibliography.

This volume is a sound, if rather favorable, study of Mrs. Leonard, certainly one of the greatest mediums in history. Like many such biographical works, it can be somewhat misleading in that it naturally concentrates upon the "hits"—and there were a great many most impressive cases in this category—and says little about the "misses," the inaccuracies, the inevitable "padding," etc. Still, it is one of the better and more comprehensive books about mediumship, and the author had the opportunity of coming to know Mrs. Leonard, a remarkably cultured, kind, and honest lady, so that her bias may be understood. Among other matters, the discussion of the Word Association Tests of Whately Carington is especially noteworthy, as are the questions of the book tests, occasional direct voice phenomena, newspaper precognition tests, and the famous Bobbie Newlove case which caused such a controversy in the mid-thirties. Since everyone who ever dealt with Mrs. Leonard was agreed upon her complete integrity and constant cooperation with all investigations, this volume is an important one to study. It can profitably be compared with Mrs. Leonard's own books about her mediumistic gift and with Alta Piper's work about her mother.

F.
Survival Issue

C. J. Ducasse, *A Critical Examination of the Belief in a Life After Death.* Charles C. Thomas, Springfield, Illinois, 1961, 318 pages, index.

A major treatment of the survival problem by one of America's most distinguished academic philosophers, the late Professor Ducasse, longtime professor at Brown University. He was renowned for his excellent grasp of psychical research, his remarkably lucid style, and the brilliant logic of his examination of philosophical matters. He brings all these talents to bear upon this vital question, and critically discusses virtually every facet, from the mind-body dualism to reincarnation. The entire work is so closely and cogently reasoned that it is imperative to read it with the greatest scrutiny; it cannot be skimmed profitably. Ducasse's work, with that of James, Broad, and Price, comprises a major part of the intellectual and philosophical capstone of psychical research, and should be undertaken only after sound and thorough preparation.

Corliss Lamont, *The Illusion of Immortality.* Introduction by John Dewey. Third Edition, Philosophical Library, New York, 1959, 278 pages, index, excellent bibliography available from the numerous footnotes.

Dr. Lamont's purpose is straightforward and unequivocal: ". . . this whole book is intended precisely to show that to believe in immortality means to *trample reason under foot* (sic)." This is possibly the most clearly presented of all anti-survivalist works. Every facet of the question is examined. Lamont argues for a monistic, humanistic viewpoint based upon the physiological and psychological findings of science which demonstrate beyond doubt, he feels, the complete unity of body, mind, and personality, hence rendering any survivable facet of man impossible. His knowledge of psychical research and spiritualism, both of which he attacks—the latter more strongly than the former—is rather sparse, and like many anti-survivalists he finds himself dubious about telepathy but forced to invoke it as an alternative in explaining the most impressive mediumistic evidence. Dr. Lamont is a very able protagonist, knowledgeable about philosophy, religion, science, and their interaction with reference to this vital issue. He writes exceedingly well, with sympathy, and without a sense of intellectual arrogance towards those who accept immortality. This is an essential book for the student concerned with survival to study in order to balance his stance. It is useful to consult Ducasse's *A Critical Examination of the Belief in a Life After Death* for his criticisms of various of Lamont's arguments.

Gardner Murphy, *Three Papers on the Survival Problem.* American Society for Psychical Research, New York, 1970, 90 pages.

This pamphlet contains reprints of three important papers first published in 1945. They are: "An Outline of Survival Evidence" in which he gives examples of the different types of evidence so far adduced; "Difficulties Confronting the Survival Hypothesis," in which Dr. Murphy considers the various loopholes—including Super ESP—in veridical information which ostensibly supports the survivalist hypothesis; and "Field Theory and Survival," in which the complex concept of field theory is considered as it might pertain to paranormal phenomena, human personality, and possible survival. These are major essays in survival research and theory which should be studied by the advanced student.

W. H. Salter, *Zoar: The Evidence of Psychical Research Concerning Survival.* Sidgwick and Jackson, London, 1961, 238 pages, index.

The late W. H. Salter was for over thirty years Hon. Secretary of the SPR; he knew most of the early group of stalwarts; he had a highly developed critical faculty and a remarkable style of writing. Added to these qualities was a strict standard of evidentiality together with a sage grasp of the limitations of quantification attempts of qualitative materials such as mediumistic communications. Based upon almost half a century of research and constant discussions with the most acute leaders in psychical research, this work is one of the most important in the field. In order to follow its argument in its subtleties and to appreciate its impact, however, one really must have a firm understanding of the principal survival evidence and the alternative explanations evinced for that evidence. Like Ducasse's work, this is a book to study and ponder.

Ian Stevenson, *Twenty Cases Suggestive of Reincarnation, Proceedings* of the American Society for Psychical Research, Volume XXVI, New York, September, 1966, 362 pages. Foreword by C. J. Ducasse.

In this scholarly study, Dr. Stevenson has presented a representative sample of the many cases whose data incline towards a reincarnationist interpretation. They are principally Oriental in origin, and this raises a very important question as to the role which cultural tendency may play in paranormal phenomena, an issue which Dr. Stevenson discusses, and which other parapsychologists, especially Gardner Murphy, have also written about. Dr. Stevenson is one of America's most eminent parapsychologists, a trained psychiatrist, and a leader in what we might term the "revival" of interest in the question of survival among psychical researchers. This work is the most significant study of reincarnation, as opposed to "discarnate survival," produced in recent years. Dr. Stevenson carries his erudition lightly and the volume is highly readable.

Additional Reading Recommended for the Advanced Student

A.
General Surveys and
Introductions to Psychical Research

Allan Angoff and B. Shaplin, Editors, *Proceedings of an International Conference: PSI Factors in Creativity.* Parapsychology Foundation, New York, 1970.

Allan Angoff, Editor, *The Psychic Force: Essays in Modern Psychical Research From The International Journal of Parapsychology,* Putnam's, New York, 1970.

Maurice Barbanell, *Spiritualism Today.* Herbert Jenkins, London, 1969.

Theodore Besterman, *Collected Papers on the Paranormal.* Helix Press, New York, 1968.

George Devereux, Editor, *Psychoanalysis and The Occult.* International Universities Press, New York, 1971; paperback: International Universities Press, New York, 1971.

Simeon Edmunds, *Spiritualism, A Critical Survey.* Aquarian Press, London, 1966.

Jule Eisenbud, *PSI and Psychoanalysis.* Grune & Stratton, New York, 1970.

Nandor Fodor, *Between Two Worlds.* Paperback Library, New York, 1969.

Nandor Fodor, *Encyclopedia of Psychic Science.* University Books, New Hyde Park, N.Y., 1966.

Sigmund Freud, *Studies in Parapsychology.* Collier-Macmillan, New York, 1963.

Eileen J. Garrett, *Awareness.* Garrett Publications, New York, 1943.

Eileen J. Garrett, Editor, *Behind the Five Senses.* J. B. Lippincott, New York, 1957.

Eileen J. Garrett, *Telepathy.* Garrett Publications, New York, 1968.

Trevor H. Hall, *The Spiritualists.* Duckworth, London, 1962; Helix Press, New York, 1963.

J. Hettinger, *Exploring The Ultra-Perceptive Faculty.* Rider, London, 1941.

J. Hettinger, *The Ultra-Perceptive Faculty.* Rider, London, 1940.

J. Arthur Hill, *Psychical Investigations.* Cassell, London, 1917.

J. Arthur Hill, *Spiritualism, Its History, Phenomena, and Doctrine.* George H. Doran Co., New York, 1919.

A. C. Holms, *The Facts of Psychic Science and Philosophy.* University Books, New Hyde Park, N.Y., 1969.

Shafica Karagulla, *Breakthrough to Creativity.* De Vorss & Co., Boston, 1956.

Andrew Lang, *Cock Lane and Common Sense.* AMS Press, New York, 1970.

R. C. LeClair, Editor, *The Letters of William James and Theodore Flournoy.* University of Wisconsin Press, Madison, Wisc., 1966.

G. K. Nelson, *Spiritualism and Society.* Schocken, New York, 1969.

Arthur W. Osborn, *The Superphysical.* Ivor Nicholson & Watson, London, 1937.

Frank Podmore, *Modern Spiritualism.* Methuen, London, 1902; recent edition: *Mediums of The 19th Century.* University Books, New Hyde Park, N.Y., 1963.

D. H. Rawcliffe, *The Psychology of The Occult.* Ridgway, New York, 1952; paperback: *Occult and Supernatural Phenomena,* Dover, New York, 1971.

J. B. Rhine, *New World of The Mind.* William Sloane & Associates, New York, 1953.

J. B. Rhine and Robert Brier, *Parapsychology Today.* Citadel Press, New York, 1968.

Joseph F. Rinn, *Searchlight on Psychical Research.* Rider, London, 1954.

L. Spence, *An Encyclopedia of Occultism.* University Books, New Hyde Park, N.Y., 1960.

Raymond Van Over and Laura Oteri, Editors, *William McDougall, Explorer of The Mind: Studies in Psychical Research.* Helix Press, New York, 1967.

G. E. Wolstenholme and E. C. P. Millar, Editors, Ciba Foundation, *Extrasensory Perception.* Little, Brown, New York, 1956; paperback: Citadel, New York, 1966.

B.
Spontaneous Phenomena

Theodore Besterman, *Crystal-Gazing: A Study in The History, Distribution, Theory, and Practice of Scrying.* University Books, New Hyde Park, N.Y., 1965.

Sir William Crookes, *Researches in The Phenomena of Spiritualism.* Psychic Book Club, London, 1953.

Eric J. Dingwall, Editor, *Abnormal Hypnotic Phenomena: A Survey of Nineteenth Century Cases.* J. & A. Churchill, London, 1967; Barnes & Noble, New York, 1968; 4 volumes.

Eric J. Dingwall and Trevor H. Hall, *Four Modern Ghosts.* London, 1958.

Eric J. Dingwall, K. M. Goldney, and Trevor H. Hall, *The Haunting of Borley Rectory.* Duckworth, London, 1956.

Jan Ehrenwald, *Telepathy and Medical Psychology.* W. W. Norton, New York, 1948.

T. Fukurai, *Clairvoyance and Thoughtography.* Rider, London, 1931.

Gustave Geley, *Clairvoyance and Materialization.* Fisher Unwin, London, 1927.

Celia Green, *Lucid Dreams.* Institute of Psychophysical Research, Oxford, 1968.

Celia Green, *Out-of-the-Body Experiences.* Institute of Psychophysical Research, Oxford, 1968.

Trevor H. Hall, *New Light on Old Ghosts.* Duckworth, London, 1965; Transatlantic, Hollywood-by-the-Sea, Fla., 1965.

Robert H. Hastings, *An Examination of the 'Borley Report,' Proceedings of the Society for Psychical Research.* Volume 55, Part 201, March, 1969.

Harry Price, *The End of Borley Rectory.* London, 1946.

Harry Price, *Rudi Schneider: A Scientific Examination of His Mediumship.* London, 1930.

William G. Roll, *The Investigation of RSPK Phenomena.* Psychical Research Foundation, Durham, N.C., 1963.

Albert von Schrenk-Notzing, *Phenomena of Materialization.* Dutton, New York, 1920.

Ian Stevenson, *Telepathic Impressions.* University of Virginia Press, Charlottesville, Va., 1970.

E. Z. Vogt and R. Hyman, *Water Witching.* U. S. A., University of Chicago Press, Chicago, 1959.

C.
Experimental and Quantitative Studies

Roberto Cavanna, Editor, *Proceedings of An International Conference on Methodology in PSI Research: PSI Favorable States of Consciousness.* Parapsychology Foundation, New York, 1970.

Roberto Cavanna and Montague Ullman, Editors, *Proceedings of An International Conference on Hypnosis, Drugs, Dreams, and PSI: PSI and Altered*

States of Consciousness. Parapsychology Foundation, New York, 1968.

Martin Ebon, Editor, *Test Your ESP.* World Publishing Co., New York, 1970; paperback: New American Library, New York, 1971.

J. G. Pratt, *On The Evaluation of Verbal Material in Parapsychology, Parapsychological Monographs No. 10.* Parapsychology Foundation, New York, 1969.

J. B. Rhine, Editor, *Progress in Parapsychology.* Parapsychology Press, Durham, N.C., 1971.

L. E. Rhine, *Manual for Introductory Experiments in Parapsychology.* Parapsychology Press, Durham, N.C., 1966.

J. H. Rush, *New Directions in Parapsychological Research, Parapsychological Monographs No. 4.* Parapsychology Foundation, New York, 1964.

Gertrude Schmeidler, *ESP in Relation to Rorschach Test Evaluation, Parapsychological Monographs No. 2.* Parapsychology Foundation, New York, 1960.

Harold Sherman, *Thoughts Through Space.* Creative Age Press, New York, 1942.

S. G. Soal, *The Experimental Situation in Psychical Research.* F. W. H. Myers Memorial Lecture, Society for Psychical Research, London, 1947.

S. G. Soal and H. T. Bowden, *The Mind Readers.* Faber, London, 1959.

Montague Ullman and Stanley Krippner, *Dream Studies and Telepathy: An Experimental Approach, Parapsychological Monographs No. 12.* Parapsychology Foundation, New York, 1970.

L. L. Vasiliev, *Experiments in Mental Suggestion.* Institute for the Study of Mental Images, Church Crookham, Hampshire, 1963.

René Warcollier, *Mind to Mind.* Creative Age Press, New York, 1948; paperback: Collier-Macmillan, New York, 1963.

D. J. West, *Tests for Extrasensory Perception: An Introductory Guide, revised edition.* Society for Psychical Research, London, 1954.

D.
Philosophical and
Religious Implications of Psychical Research

Donald H. Andrews, *The Symphony of Life.* Unity Books, Lee's Summit, Mo., 1966.

Henri Bergson, *Matter and Memory.* Macmillan, New York, 1911.

C. D. Broad, *The Mind and Its Place in Nature.* Harcourt, Brace & Co., London, 1949.

Richard M. Bucke, *Cosmic Consciousness, revised edition.* University Books, New Hyde Park, N.Y., 1961; paperback: Dutton, New York, 1969; Citadel, New York, 1970.

Sir Cyril Burt, *Psychology and Psychical Research.* Seventeenth F. W. H. Myers Memorial Lecture, Society for Psychical Research, London, 1968.

Whately Carington, *Matter, Mind, and Meaning.* Methuen, London, 1949; Books for Libraries, Freeport, N.Y., 1970.

Alexis Carrel, *Man, The Unknown.* Harper & Bros., New York, 1935.

W. H. Clark, *Chemical Ecstasy: Psychedelic Drugs and Religion.* New York, Sheed and Ward, 1969.

J. W. Dunne, *An Experiment With Time, third edition.* Hillery, New York, 1958; paperback: Princeton, 1955.

Antony Flew, Editor, *Body, Mind, and Death.* Macmillan, New York, 1964.

Gustave Geley, *From the Unconscious to the Conscious.* William Collins, London, 1920.

Paul L. Higgins, *Encountering the Unseen.* T. W. Denison, Minneapolis, 1966.

Thomson J. Hudson, *The Law of Psychic Phenomena: A Working Hypothesis for the Systematic Study of Hypnotism, Spiritism, Mental Therapeutics.* Hudson-Cohan, Chicago, 1970.

Raynor C. Johnson, *Watcher on The Hills.* Hodder & Stoughton, London, 1959.

C. G. Jung, *The Interpretation of Nature and The Psyche.* Princeton University Press, Princeton, 1955.

R. E. L. Masters and J. Houston, *The Varieties of Psychedelic Experience.* Holt, Rinehart, and Winston, New York, 1966; paperback: Dell, New York, 1967.

Arthur W. Osborn, *The Future is Now: The Significance of Precognition.* University Books, New Hyde Park, N.Y., 1962.

J. B. Rhine, *Telepathy and Human Personality.* The Tenth F. W. H. Myers Memorial Lecture, Society for Psychical Research, London, 1950.

J. R. Smythies, Editor, *Brain and Mind: Modern Concepts of The Nature of Mind.* Routledge Kegan Paul, London, 1967.

J. H. M. Whiteman, *The Mystical Life.* Faber & Faber, London, 1961.

E.
Mediumship

M. Bouisseau, *The Life of A Sensitive.* Sidgwick & Jackson, London, 1955.

Geraldine Cummins, *Unseen Adventures.* Rider, London, 1951.

Eric J. Dingwall and Harry Price, *Revelations of A Spirit Medium.* London, 1922.

Theodore Flournoy, *From India to The Planet Mars.* University Books, New Hyde Park, N.Y., 1963.

E. W. Fornell, *The Unhappy Medium: Spiritualism and The Life of Margaret Fox.* University of Texas Press, Austin, 1964.

Emma Hardinge, *Modern American Spiritualism: A Twenty Years' Record of The Communion Between Earth and The World of Spirits.* University Books, New Hyde Park, N.Y., 1970.

Peter Hurkos, *Psychic: The Story of Peter Hurkos.* Bobbs-Merrill, Indianapolis, 1961.

J. Leasor, *The Millioneth Chance: The Story of The R 101.* Hamish Hamilton, London, 1957.

Gladys Osborne Leonard, *Brief Darkness.* Cassel & Co., London, 1931.

Gladys Osborne Leonard, *The Last Crossing.* Cassel & Co., London, 1937.

A. Muhl, *Automatic Writing.* Helix Press, New York, 1964.

Ira Progoff, *The Image of An Oracle.* Helix Press, New York, 1964.

W. H. Salter, *Trance Mediumship.* Society for Psychical Research, London, 1950.

F.
Survival Issue

C. D. Broad, *Human Identity and Survival.* F. W. H. Myers Memorial Lecture, Society for Psychical Research, London, 1958.

Hereward Carrington, *The Case for Psychic Survival.* Citadel Press, New York, 1957.

Jacques Choron, *Modern Man and Mortality.* Macmillan, New York, 1964.

Geraldine Cummins, *Beyond Human Personality.* Psychic Press, London, 1952.

Geraldine Cummins, *The Road to Immortality.* L. S. A. Publications, London, 1947.

E. R. Dodds, "Why I do not believe in survival," *Proceedings* of The Society for Psychical Research. Volume XLII: pp. 147-72, 1934.

C. J. Ducasse, *Nature, Mind, and Death.* Open Court Publishing Co., La Salle, Ill., 1951.

Herman Feifel, Editor, *The Meaning of Death.* McGraw-Hill, New York, 1959.

Camille Flammarion, *Death and Its Mystery,* London, 1922.

Sir Oliver Lodge, *The Survival of Man, eleventh edition.* Methuen, London, 1927.

Karlis Osis, *Deathbed Observations by Physicians and Nurses, Parapsychological Monographs No. 3.* Parapsychology Foundation, New York, 1961.

C. Drayton Thomas, *In The Dawn Beyond Death.* Lectures Universal, Ltd., London, 1959.

Arnold Toynbee et al., *Man's Concern With Death.* Hodder & Stoughton, London, 1968.

Una, Lady Troubridge, *The Life and Death of Radclyffe-Hall.* Hammond, London, 1961.

Nea Walker, *The Bridge.* Cassell, London, 1927.

Nea Walker, *Through A Stranger's Hands.* Hutchinson, London, 1935.

Leslie D. Weatherhead, *The Manner of The Resurrection in The Light of Modern Science and Psychical Research.* Abingdon Press, New York, 1959.

Stewart Edward White and Harwood White, *Across The Unknown.* E. P. Dutton, New York, 1939.

Stewart Edward White, *The Betty Book.* E. P. Dutton, New York, 1937.

Stewart Edward White, *The Unobstructed Universe.* E. P. Dutton, New York, 1940.

Carl Wickland, *Thirty Years Among the Dead.* Spiritualist Press, London, 1949.

CHAPTER FOUR

PROCEDURES FOR SITTING WITH A MEDIUM

Every serious student of psi will wish to experience paranormal phenomena personally, and the most readily available possibility is a series of "sittings" with mediums. A very large part of the most important and impressive evidence for psi collected during the ninety years of psychical research consists in records of such sittings, and the student can, therefore, not only further his own studies but may well add to the general knowledge of the discipline. As Professor Thouless of Cambridge has wisely observed, psychical research is one of the very few fields left in which the careful and knowledgeable amateur can still advance the frontier of knowledge.

It is imperative that the student have a good grasp of the basic understanding so far gained of mediumship and that he has realistic expectations before beginning his work with mediums. Many have undertaken mediumistic experiences with overly optimistic and simplistic goals and have been sorely disappointed. Some of the possible pitfalls are discussed in this chapter, and many more detailed references can be found in the literature annotated in the Bibliographies.

Probably the most common hope among individuals at sittings is to gain conviction that a loved one does survive death as a self-conscious, articulate, remembering personality. Each will have to decide for himself of what convincing evidence would consist and how important would be the corroborative opinion of others who might view the evidence in a less subjective fashion. Paul Beard has made an enlightening distinction in his *Survival of Death* between "conviction" which can only be personal, and "proof" which can be public. Fifty years ago, the Nobel Prize-winning physiologist Charles Richet, a pioneer in research into physical phenomena, ruefully remarked that phenomena which were overwhelmingly evidential during a sitting melted into inconsequentialities when discussed with someone who had not been present: in a curious way, the doubts of the one who had not experienced the phenomena undercut the direct observations of the one who had. It was as though someone returning from a trip and describing what he had seen found that his chair-bound listener by his non-experiential disbelief convinced the traveler that he had never really visited foreign lands at all. This factor demonstrates graphically that in order for mediumistic evidence to carry sufficient weight vicariously for the non-experient, it must be of a very high order of evidentiality and consist of items which lie between the innanely trivial and the innanely general. Needless to say, such evidence is rare.

The gap between what seems "possible" in our commonsense world and what psi phenomena seem to be is so great that most people naturally assume that reports of psi must be erroneous, fraudulent, or illusory. The student must be prepared for this reaction; and, of course, must himself consider in the case of each phenomenon whether, in fact, anything paranormal has occurred. In order to satisfy himself that paranormality is the correct cause for the phenomenon, the student must eliminate all normal causes as underlying the occurrence. This is notoriously difficult to do, and the student may find that the best that can be done is to reduce the normal possibilities to collusion or fraud; the weighing of the probability of these as causes is a matter for very great care, and only considerable experience together with a constantly alert and judicious attitude can lead to sound conclusions.

It will be recalled from the brief description of sensitives in the opening chapter that there are several types: clairvoyant, clairaudient, clairsentient, direct voice, trance, and physical whose ostensible phenomena may be of varying kinds. Many clairvoyant, clairaudient, or clairsentient mediums use a "token object" in a psychometric way to begin their sittings. Because physical mediums are rare today, those precautions and possible controls one should maintain in investigating them are not dealt with here. For a good discussion of this and other aspects of the subject, the pamphlet "Hints on Sitting with Mediums," available from The Society for Psychical Research (London), is highly recommended.

Sensitives vary in their personal views as to the sources of any veridical information they impart to sitters. Some feel that all data emanate from discarnates; others that much is due to some form of ESP, and relatively little due to surviving spirits; and still others that much of a personal and advisory nature may be derived by precognition and telepathy while really evidential material demonstrating survival is provided by discarnates. The student will probably find that a very large proportion of what the average medium says will fall into the category of personal information and advice and that many mediums will feel that this "reading" does not come from discarnates. A medium may ask the sitter if there is a particular person "on the other side" he wishes to try to reach, in which case the medium will try to perceive discarnates rather than gain information paranormally from the sitter or other living persons.

How to Locate a Medium

In the United States, there are few sensitives who are not connected with the National Spiritualist Association of Churches, 11811 Watertown Plank Road, Milwaukee, Wisconsin 53226; and the NSAC can provide lists of approved mediums, spiritualist churches, and state or local spiritualist societies. In Great Britain, the Spiritualist Association of Great Britain, 33 Belgrave Square, London, S.W. 1, holds mediumistic sittings by a large number of mediums daily in its headquarters and can give names and addresses of mediums and churches throughout Great Britain. The College of Psychic Studies, 16 Queensberry Place, S.W. 7, also can arrange for sittings with several approved mediums. One may also often find local spiritualist churches listed in the telephone directory.

While dealing with both mediums and non-mediumistic spiritualists, one must always remember that spiritualism is a religion and its adherents naturally believe in its principles. They have generally proven very helpful and cooperative with open-minded students; but it cannot be overly emphasized that because they are personally convinced of the reality of discarnate communication and because this belief undergirds their religion, one asking for assistance in learning about mediumistic phenomena must be neither irreverent, scoffing, nor discourteous.

How to Arrange a Sitting

It is always best to preserve anonymity when making an appointment for a sitting. This insures that the medium does not face the charge that she may have checked on the sitter or have noted recent deaths of relatives in obituary columns, etc. It also makes any veridical information one does obtain more evidential, because one possibly normal explanation has been eliminated. When one does have to give a name, a pseudonym can be used. Promptness in keeping the sitting appointment is important, for mediums frequently have a heavy schedule and tardiness will inconvenience not only the medium but all subsequent sitters.

The Sitter's Conduct During a Sitting

The sitter's principal aims must be to encourage the medium, to clarify points when really essential, and to cooperate fully in order to obtain optimum results. Simultaneously, to increase the possibility of evidential material, one must avoid inadvertently giving the medium information either during any conversation preceding the sitting or during the sitting itself. One must not volunteer information or answer the medium's questions any more fully than is absolutely necessary. Some mediums, either consciously or unconsciously, "fish" for data by means of shrewd but simple questions and then construct, through a series of such questions, an apparently impressive item of evidential information. Frequently, the sitter is totally unaware that this process has produced the item. Therefore, nothing is more important than a *full, verbatim* record of the sitting, including both the medium's and the sitter's words. Obviously, the best means is a tape recorder, and most good mediums are amenable to its use, so long as it is set up beforehand and does not disturb them by its noise or by the sitter's manipulating it during the sitting.

There are several advantages of the taped record over either a stenographic one or notes by the sitter. First, the nuances of phrases and the tone of voices of both sitter and medium are faithfully recorded for evaluation. Such facets of the sitting can have considerable bearing upon the quality of the material. Second, the tape recorder avoids the presence of a third person which can further inhibit the medium and possibly confuse the phenomena, some of which may be inadvertently directed to the recorder rather than to the sitter. Third, the tape recorder frees the sitter to pay full and close attention to the medium so that facial expressions, gestures, and movements may be noted and utilized in judging the sitting.

If a tape recorder is not available and a stenographer is, be sure that the stenographer is experienced in mediumistic sittings, is a person who will not interfere in any way during the sitting, and will be as calm and unobtrusive as possible.

A prospective sitter can easily appreciate that to help the medium in establishing the best conditions and still not divulge information is by no means an easy task. Some, in their determination to succeed in the first aim are overly verbose and chat away amicably, providing the medium with all sorts of information upon which she may, unconsciously and unwittingly, base later "messages." Responsible mediums do not want such gratis data, for the veridical nature of *all* the evidence is placed in doubt or rejected entirely. Other sitters, determined not "to give anything away," refuse to respond to either questions or to actually veridical information; they may constantly interrupt the medium with questions, or they may contradict and argue with her. Clearly, such behavior confuses, distracts, and annoys the medium; and it is hardly surprising that such sitters rarely do receive evidential data. They then congratulate themselves upon a "successful" sitting because they have "proved" that the whole matter is bunkum. The experienced sitter avoids both of these extremes.

Some who begin sitting with mediums are most disappointed at how little material that is veridical or even pertinent is obtained. If one considers, however, that, supposing some people may survive death, the means of communication must be very different and very difficult compared with the normal physical means to which we are accustomed, it is not remarkable that one receives so little, but that one may receive anything at all which seems to indicate a discarnate communicator. Sitters will probably find that, even with a highly talented medium, most of her "communications" may be chaff and not wheat. Thus, other attributes one must cultivate are patience and perseverence. Nor should one ignore the apparently fruitless sittings: first, because occasionally in looking through the records of such sittings, one may be later struck by an item that had no meaning at the time but later has proven significant; second, because unless one keeps full records of *all* sittings, of whatever quality, one cannot fairly and accurately assess the mediumistic material one has obtained. Instead, one tends to recall only the "hits" or pertinent items, and to forget all the "misses."

With mediums who are awake while demonstrating psi, one should behave as already outlined. In the case of a trance medium, one must, in addition, take care to follow her instructions and be quiet while she is entering and leaving the trance state; otherwise, the medium may become distressed or even ill.

It may happen that the medium finds it impossible, for some reason, to demonstrate her psi with a sitter. An honest medium will frankly say so, for she knows that whatever the psi faculty may be, it is not, at this juncture at least, dependable or controllable. Any medium who claims that she can *guarantee* paranormal manifestations is a medium to avoid: she is either dishonest or extremely naïve and prone to imagining psi phenomena rather than producing them.

Judging the Mediumistic Material

In determining the veridical or non-veridical nature of items recorded in a sitting, there are various important factors to be taken into account. The accuracy and completeness of the records are, of course, of fundamental significance. All else depends upon them. In the absence of a verbatim record, many, if not all, sitters tend to overestimate the quantity and quality of material received, forgetting the inaccuracies which may well greatly outweigh the sound information. Thorough tests of the observational accuracy of experienced sitters at contrived sittings where planned actions and demonstrations of objects took place have conclusively shown how low such skills generally are. One can easily test this for oneself. Following a sitting, write down *in order* all the items of whatever evidential value you recall as fully as possible. Then check this list with your tape recording or verbatim report. You will find great discrepancies, in all probability. The vital importance of complete and accurate records cannot be overly stressed. Without them, the student has no sound means of verifying or rejecting items nor any factual basis for conclusions.

As explained earlier, the theoretical possibility of "Super ESP" means that any veridical information cannot be conclusive proof of a surviving personality as the source. Yet in view of the general lack of experimental data substantiating such a far-reaching, controlled, selective psi faculty, some feel that one may be justified in viewing this theoretical obstacle as somewhat remote; others hold that until this possibility has been eliminated (and there is so far no way of doing so) this explanation must take precedence over that of a discarnate communicator. Each student must come to his own conclusion regarding the issue. In any case, if one eliminates Super ESP, there remains telepathy between the medium and either the sitter or another person present, clairvoyance, precognition, psychokinesis, coincidence, chance, unintentional sensory clues or information from the sitter, or fraud. The likelihood of many of these is lessened if one can arrange a "proxy sitting," i.e., one in which a third party sits with the medium on behalf of someone else who is not present and is unknown to the medium.   Usually, some "token object" belonging to the person for whom the sitting is held is given the medium to assist her to "tune in" on that person. This kind of experiment, however, should only be arranged after one is fully familiar with the procedures of a sitting, after one is fairly certain of the rapport with and the quality of the medium involved, and if one has as proxy a fully experienced sitter. It is essential that the medium know beforehand that such a proxy sitting is going to be held and that she give her consent.

One means of judging the validity and pertinence of the material is to break it down into separate items, list them in order, and then ask several other people unknown to the medium and ignorant of the identity of the sitter to mark whether the items pertain to themselves, for whom the sitting was neither held nor intended. In such a "cross-matching" procedure, if there is a high incidence of pertinence, this demonstrates that the given item is so general that it could fit many people and its evidentiality is, consequently, non-existent. Sitters will frequently find that a large proportion of the items fall into this category.

There are more precise quantitative procedures for evaluating qualitative material, and interested students are referred to J. G. Pratt and W. R. Birge, "Appraising verbal test material in parapsychology," *Journal of Parapsychology,* Volume 12, 1948, pp. 236-256; J. G. Pratt, *On the Evaluation of Verbal Material in Parapsychology, Parapsychological Monographs No. 10,* Parapsychology Foundation, New York, 1969; and D. S. Burdick and W. G. Roll, "Differential Weighting of ESP Responses," *Journal A. S. P. R.,* Volume 65, April, 1971, pp. 173-184. One may also obtain expert advice regarding such evaluation from either The American Society for Psychical Research, The Society for Psychical Research (London), or a department of parapsychology at a university.

Conclusion

Very frequent criticisms of mediumistic material, whatever its source, are that it is either so general as to be platitudinous or so trivial as to be meaningless. There is certainly a very sound basis for these points; however, in fairness, one must add that if the purpose of sitting is to determine whether a loved one survives death, it is essential that the ostensibly surviving personality prove that it is in fact the loved one, and how can that be done except through trivia i. e., precisely described persons, events, or objects which seem of little import themselves, but may be unique to the sitter and the deceased loved one? Second, if one also hopes to learn something of the nature of the afterlife, if there be one, such descriptions would surely vary in terms of the background and viewpoint of the "communicating spirit," and would doubtless include generalities about the religious, ethical, and metaphysical characteristics of life, both earthly and post-mortem, as viewed by a specific discarnate personality. When one considers, moreover, how large a percentage of our daily conversation falls into the category of either trivial or platitudinous, if there be survival, it may well be unrealistic to expect a marked raising of the level of communication on the part of a given individual.

However many the pitfalls and disappointments in sittings, they remain an important phase of the student's investigations; only through direct experience can one learn to evaluate the great mass of mediumistic evidence soundly; such sittings give the student firsthand experience with what may be paranormal phenomena; and, if the student is fortunate enough to obtain some highly evidential items, he will soon perceive both how impressive they can be personally, and how rapidly their impact diminishes upon those who have not had such personal results. All of these lessons are important.

Nowhere in psychical research is the balanced, judicious, open-minded attitude so vital as in arranging, conducting, and evaluating mediumistic sittings. They can be puzzling, frustrating, irritating, exciting, and, sometimes, moving. We seem to be in a very different world from our hectic, commonsense one, and perhaps, just perhaps, we may be.

CHAPTER FIVE

RESOURCES AVAILABLE TO THE STUDENT

In this chapter students will find information about research societies and foundations, other organizations related to psychical research, libraries with strong holdings in the discipline's literature, publications of importance, and a note about bookshops. All of the information was determined to be as accurate as possible at the time of compilation, but such items as subscription rates or membership dues might be somewhat changed. In any case, the student should direct his inquiries to the appropriate organization at the address given for full details. All of the organizations listed welcome those who are seriously interested in psychical research and students should not hesitate to investigate membership possibilities; indeed, they should support the research and information activities by membership in the societies and any related groups in which they are interested.

1.
Research Organizations in the United Kingdom

The Society for Psychical Research, 1 Adam & Eve Mews, London, W. 8.

Formed in 1882 under the leadership of Sir William Barrett, F. W. H. Myers, Henry Sidgwick, and other leading scholars, the SPR has as its purposes: "to examine without prejudice or prepossession and in a scientific spirit those faculties of man, real or supposed, which appear to be inexplicable on any generally recognized hypothesis." During ninety years, the Society has done precisely that with a level of scholarship, critical standards of evidence, and integrity which will stand comparison with any research organization of whatever discipline. Its *Journal* and *Proceedings,* together with monographs and significant lectures which it reproduces, are possibly the most important sources in English of raw material for the student of psychical research. The Society, in order to maintain its utter impartiality, does not hold any "corporate views," but publishes material of contradictory opinions, so long as they are scholarly.

An annual Membership subscription of $7.50 entitles the Member to the use of the excellent library, admission to the monthly lectures, and copies of the *Journal* and *Proceedings.* The SPR welcomes members from any country, and since its publications are essential reading for the serious student, he will find it well worthwhile to join, thereby obtaining them and further strengthening the support for psychical research. All inquiries regarding membership or publications should be directed to the Secretary at the above address.

2.

Research Organizations in the United States

The American Society for Psychical Research, 5 West 73rd Street, New York, New York 10023.

First formed in 1885, the ASPR is one of the major research bodies in the world dealing with paranormal phenomena. It collects and investigates reports of spontaneous phenomena, supports research into experimentation and quantitative analysis, has studied the claims of numerous mediums, and is concerned with any and all aspects of psychical research. The Society's standards in research are most rigorous and scientific, as befits a group of scholars devoted to critical investigation and analysis. It maintains one of the finest libraries in the field, the use of which is open to Members, Fellows, and bonafide scholars. It presents lectures and cooperates with similar bodies in other countries. The annual Membership fee is $15, which entitles the Member to a copy of the *Journal* and *Proceedings.* A Fellow pays a fee of $25 which entitles him to certain library privileges in addition to those of the Member. A special Student Membership rate for full-time students only is available at $10 for two years. (One year Student Membership is not available.)

The *Journal* is published in January, April, July, and October. *Proceedings* are published irregularly and contain reports of greater length and of special interest. The *Newsletter* is published four times a year and deals with brief news items of general information about research, lectures, and other activities of the ASPR and its members.

For any information about membership, publications, and activities of the ASPR, direct inquiries to the ASPR at the above address. Since the ASPR is the leading research society in the United States, serious students of psychical research should find it very advantageous to join and will, furthermore, by their membership, help increase the much needed support for the continuation and expansion of psychical research.

Foundation for Research on the Nature of Man, Box 6846, College Station, Durham, North Carolina 27708.

The FRNM was established by Dr. J. B. Rhine when he retired from Duke University. There are two aspects to the Foundation so far: The Institute for Parapsychology which continues the research of the Parapsychology Laboratory at Duke University which Dr. Rhine directed for so many years; and the Parapsychology Press which publishes *The Journal of Parapsychology* as well as monographs from time to time.

The Journal of Parapsychology is published in March, June, September, and December. Subscription rates are $8 for one year, $15 for two years, and $20 for three years; single current issues are $2. One of the principal scholarly journals in the field, especially in terms of quantitative work, the advanced student in particular should be familiar with it.

The Parapsychological Association.

This is an international society of professional parapsychologists founded in 1957 to enable them to hold annual meetings and exchange views. Its membership is not open to the general public. The Parapsychological Association was accepted as an Associate of The American Association for the Advancement of Science in 1969 which indicated that its standards of scholarship met the highest criteria. This step has greatly enhanced not only this particular Association's prestige, but that of the discipline which it represents, and is one of the most encouraging signs of changing public and scientific attitudes towards psychical research.

Only recently the *Proceedings of The Parapsychological Association,* edited by W. G. Roll, have become available to the public. Volumes 1-4, covering the first ten international conventions, can be obtained from: *Proceedings* of The Parapsychological Association, Duke Station, Durham, North Carolina 27706. These volumes cover reports from many countries upon a very wide range of topics. Prices: $12 for the four volumes hardback, $6 paperback; individual volumes are $3.50 each hardback, $1.95 each paperback. These volumes are well worth purchasing for the advanced student and for anyone who wishes to build a sound personal library in psychical research.

The Parapsychology Foundation, Inc., 29 West 57th Street, New York, New York 10019.

Established in 1951 by the late Mrs. Eileen Garrett, the Foundation has aimed to support research into all facets of ESP and paranormal phenomena. It has held international conferences of scholars from many different disciplines such as psychology, psychiatry, physics, pharmacology, medicine, religion, and physiology, as well as parapsychology. It has published important monographs covering research it has supported—the series of *Parapsychological Monographs;* for ten years it published the *International Journal of Parapsychology;* its *Proceedings* cover material presented at its international conferences; its bimonthly *Parapsychology Review* (which replaced the *Newsletter* in 1970) keeps researchers and interested laymen abreast of work and activities around the world; it has published books, and for several years, the Foundation published a popular magazine, *Tomorrow,* dealing with matters of psychical research. It has maintained one of the leading libraries in parapsychological materials open to bona fide students; and it has periodically supported publications of very different types in Great Britain, France, Switzerland, and Italy. Its own Division of Research also undertook important work upon the survival issue, mediumistic phenomena, the use of certain drugs to stimulate ESP, etc.

If the student is interested further, he should write the Foundation for information about its current activities and subscription to the *Parapsychology Review.*

Psychical Research Foundation, Inc., Duke Station, Durham, North Carolina 27708.

The Foundation was established for the purpose of investigating evidence for survival, and Mr. W. G. Roll is Project Director. The personnel and facilities of the Foundation have recently been expanded, and it is anticipated that it will be feasible to investigate more cases and launch more experimentation bearing upon its prime purpose. The Foundation publishes a quarterly bulletin, *Theta,* dealing with current research on the survival problem and book reviews of pertinent works. The annual subscription is $1.50. This is an excellent and inexpensive manner in which to keep abreast of survival research, which is rapidly expanding.

3.
Libraries in the United Kingdom

Students interested in using any of the libraries listed should enquire at the library regarding permission and the regulations covering such use. They will find the personnel connected with these libraries most cooperative and helpful. This listing is not necessarily exhaustive of significant collections.

The Churches' Fellowship for Psychical and Spiritual Studies, 5 Denison House, Vauxhall Bridge Road, London, S.W. 1.

Approximately 2000 volumes. Strongest in the Christian approach to psychical research, healing, prayer, and mysticism. This Library was closed temporarily in the autumn of 1971 due to lease problems and the student should enquire at the Secretary's office, 88 Newman Street, London W1P 3LD, phone: 01-636 3469 for information about the use of the library.

The College of Psychic Studies, 16 Queensberry Place, London, S.W. 7.

Approximately 11,000 volumes. Especially strong on all phases of spiritualism, the religious aspects of psi, healing, meditation, etc., as well as in esoteric traditions. A fairly good section on psychical research is being steadily built up. The principal research publications are subscribed to, although not all back issues are available.

The Greater World Christian Spiritualist League, 5, Lansdowne Road, London, W. 11.

Approximately 2,000 volumes, mostly upon spiritualist topics.

The Harry Price Collection, London University, Senate House Library, London, W.C. 1.

15,000 volumes left to the University by the late researcher and writer. Access is by permission of the librarian in charge of the collection. Very strong in legerdemain, witchcraft, and physical phenomena studies. Few additions since the later 1930's.

The Society for Psychical Research, 1 Adam & Eve Mews, London, W. 8.

Approximately 10,000 volumes. One of the principal libraries of the world on psychical research as a discipline, mediumistic studies and files of primary materials, plus coverage of European research and publications. Open to Members and to bona fide researchers.

The Spiritualist Association of Great Britain, 33 Belgrave Square, London, S.W. 1.

Approximately 4,000 volumes, mostly on spiritualist matters.

The Theosophical Society, 50 Gloucester Place, London, W. 1.

About 13,000 volumes. Excellent coverage of the general field, with special strengths in theosophy, occultism, and eastern philosophy.

4.

Libraries in the United States

Students interested in using any of the libraries listed should inquire at the library regarding permission and the regulations covering such use. They will find the personnel connected with these libraries most cooperative and helpful. This listing is not necessarily exhaustive of significant collections.

The American Society for Psychical Research, 5 West 73rd Street, New York, New York 10023.

Approximately 6,000 volumes. This is one of the best collections of materials on psychical research in the world. It is open to Members and to bona fide researchers.

Parapsychology Foundation, 29 West 57th Street, New York, New York 10019.

Approximately 7500 volumes. The Eileen J. Garrett Library is especially strong in post-1930 literature. A periodical index covering articles since 1966 is in progress of being compiled. There is a very full collection of learned periodicals from many countries. The Library is for reference only and no volumes may be removed from the premises. It is open to the public from 9 A.M. to 5 P.M. Monday through Friday.

Spiritual Frontiers Fellowship, Inc., 800 Custer Avenue, Suite Number 1, Evanston, Illinois 60202.

Approximately 5,000 volumes. This library's holdings include many works on psychical research, but it is especially strong upon the religious and philosophical aspects, healing, prayer, and mysticism. Most of its books are available through mail to members of SFF.

5.
Publications in the United Kingdom

Details about subscription rates may be obtained from the offices of the organization producing the publication. These organizations also occasionally publish pamphlets, lectures, and monographs which may be of interest to the student.

The Churches' Fellowship for Psychical and Spiritual Studies Quarterly Review. Published in March, June, September, and December, This quarterly covers the activities of the many branches of the Fellowship, articles pertaining to the relationship between psychic phenomena and Christianity, healing, prayer, plus book reviews of works that fall within the purview of the Fellowship's particular interests. Address enquiries to the General Secretary, Churches' Fellowship for Psychical and Spiritual Studies, 88 Newman Street, London W1P 3LD.

Light, A Journal of Psychic Studies. Published in March, June, September, and December. *Light* is concerned with any and all aspects of psychical studies, from the experimental to the religious significance of psi, but its emphasis is upon the latter. Founded in 1881, *Light* was for many years a spiritualist journal, but its viewpoints are much wider now, although by no means of the scientific nature to be found in the *SPR Journal.* Address enquiries to The College of Psychic Studies, 16 Queensberry Place, London, S.W. 7.

Journal of the Society For Psychical Research. Published in March, June, September, and December. Probably the most prestigious of all journals in the field, its approach is highly critical, scholarly, and erudite. Articles concern experimentation, reports of spontaneous phenomena, theoretical discussions, and re-assessments of earlier works. The book reviews are of a very high quality.

Proceedings of The Society for Psychical Research. Published irregularly, these volumes contain more lengthy articles and studies than the *Journal* could accommodate, but with as high a standard.

Address enquiries about these publications, as well as the numerous pamphlets the SPR has available to The Secretary, The Society for Psychical Research, 1 Adam & Eve Mews, London, W. 8.

6.
Publications in the United States

Details about subscription rates may be obtained from the offices of the publication or of the organization which produces the publication. These organizations also occasionally publish pamphlets, lectures, and monographs which may be of interest to the student.

Journal of the American Society for Psychical Research. Published in January, April, July and October. A larger publication than the *SPR's Journal,* this is equally erudite and a principal source of information about current research, theories, and controversies in parapsychology, as well as containing excellent book reviews.

Proceedings of the American Society for Psychical Research. Published irregularly, these volumes contain more lengthy articles and studies than the *Journal* could accommodate, but with as high a standard.

Address inquiries about these publications, as well as the pamphlets the ASPR has available, to The American Society for Psychical Research, 5 West 73rd Street, New York, New York 10023.

Journal of Parapsychology. Published in March, June, September, and December. This journal specializes in quantitative experimental articles, although many others are also printed, together with fine book reviews. This is a vital source of data about research in the laboratory.

Address inquiries to The Editor, *Journal of Parapsychology,* Foundation for Research on the Nature of Man, Box 6846, College Station, Durham, North Carolina 27708.

Parapsychology Review. Published bimonthly. This contains some larger articles, but much of its material is in the form of news items about a wide variety of activities in psychical research around the world, recent library acquisitions at the Eileen J. Garrett Library, and book reviews. Probably the best manner of keeping abreast of the manifold facets of the growing discipline internationally is through this publication. Address inquiries to The Parapsychology Foundation, Inc., 29 West 57th Street, New York, New York 10019.

Psychic. Published bimonthly. A popular magazine designed to present sound information about psychical research, its ancillary fields and its ramifications in a manner easily read and grasped by the man in the street. During the three years it has been published, it has maintained a high level of material and of production. Its aim seems similar to that of Mrs. Eileen Garrett's now defunct *Tomorrow*.

Address inquiries to *Psychic,* The Bolen Company, 680 Beach Street, San Francisco, California 94109.

Spiritual Frontiers. Published quarterly in the winter, spring, summer, and autumn. Now two years old, this replaced the smaller *Gateway* which SFF had produced for some years. The journal encompasses a wide range of topics and includes articles by parapsychologists, but its emphasis is upon the religious and philosophical significance of psychical research within the Christian context.

Address inquiries to Spiritual Frontiers Fellowship, Inc., 800 Custer Avenue, Suite Number 1, Evanston, Illinois 60202.

Theta. Published quarterly, this is not a magazine, but a bulletin of six to eight pages dealing with recent research and books bearing upon the survival issue. As such, it is an excellent and inexpensive way of keeping abreast of survival research. Annual subscription is $1.50.

Address inquiries to The Psychical Research Foundation, Duke Station, Durham, North Carolina 27708.

7.
Organizations Related to Psychical Research in the United Kingdom

There are a great many occult and esoteric groups interested in psi phenomena in connection with certain traditions or approaches; but this volume does not deal with the occult and they are not, therefore, listed.

The Churches' Fellowship for Psychical and Spiritual Studies, 88 Newman Street, London, W1P 3LD. Founded in 1954 by clergy and laymen to study the paranormal and ESP in relation to church teaching, it numbers among its patrons twenty-one Anglican Bishops and many leading members of the Free Churches. While Full Membership is restricted to those who belong to a church affiliated with the World Council of Churches, Associate Membership is open to all those genuinely seeking a deeper knowledge of paranormal phenomena. The Fellowship has specialist research groups in psychical phenomena, healing, mysticism, meditation, and mental health, approximately one hundred study groups throughout the country, yearly conferences, a library with postal service, and a journal.

For further information, write the General Secretary at the above address.

The College of Psychic Studies, 16 Queensberry Place, London, S.W. 7. Established in 1884 as the London Spiritualist Alliance, the College is now a body without any corporate viewpoint, welcoming to membership anyone interested in psychical research or related fields. It has a large library, holds weekly lectures upon a wide variety of subjects, arranges sittings with approved mediums, holds courses dealing with many topics, is concerned with healing, meditation, etc. Recently, it has become involved in some research projects as well. While it is not a research-oriented organization like the SPR, the College is interested in all activities which shed light upon psychical matters. It welcomes members from overseas. Advantages of membership include the use of all College facilities, a free subscription to *Light,* and reduced fees for sittings with mediums, lectures, and courses.

Full information may be obtained from the General Secretary of the College at the above address.

Spiritualist Association of Great Britain, 33 Belgrave

Square, London, S.W. 1. The SAGB holds daily sittings of mediums, both individually and in groups, demonstrations of clairvoyance, healing sessions, circles for development of mediumship, etc. There are various kinds of membership available, including daily membership for visitors—one must be a member of SAGB in order to use the facilities or attend sittings with mediums. There is a library and a bookshop.

Information may be obtained from the SAGB at the address given above.

8.
Organizations Related to Psychical Research in the United States

There are dozens of occult and esoteric groups which have interest in psi phenomena in one fashion or another, but as indicated earlier, this work does not deal with the occult traditions. The spiritualist movement does not have the strong centralization in the United States as it does with the SAGB in London. Consequently, the student does not have the same opportunity for observation of many mediums in one location unless he attends one of the spiritualist camps held mostly during the summer in various parts of the country; but some of these camps have, on occasion, been plagued with exposures of fraudulent mediums so that great care must be exercised.

Spiritual Frontiers Fellowship, 800 Custer Avenue, Suite Number One, Evanston, Illinois 60202.

Established in 1956 by a group of clergymen and laymen encouraged by the formation of the Churches' Fellowship for Psychical and Spiritual Studies in Great Britain, the aims of SFF include investigation of the relationship between the paranormal and Christianity, the religious significance of the findings of psychical research, the mystical tradition, prayer, spiritual healing, and the issue of survival. There are a large number of groups for study throughout the country, an annual meeting, library and book services, and a periodic newsletter. Membership is open to anyone concerned with these aims, and details may be obtained by writing the Executive Secretary at the address above.

9.
Bookshops for Works in Psychical Research

While many bookshops have some works dealing with psychical research, most are either general bookshops or tend to specialize in occult and esoteric books rather than in psychical research literature. Consequently, the personnel may not be fully conversant with the field. As noted earlier, some of the organizations offer book purchasing services for their members. Probably the best source for books dealing with psychical research in the United Kingdom is Watkins Bookshop, 19 and 21 Cecil Court, Charing Cross Road, London, W.C. 2. Watkins has been a specialist shop in books of this kind, as well as in occult and mystical works, for many years, and there is a mail order service not only within the United Kingdom but overseas as well. In the United States, the leading bookshop in this field is Samuel Weiser, Inc., 734 Broadway, New York, New York 10003. Samuel Weiser has a very large stock of works in psychical research, a knowledgeable staff to assist students with their needs, and a mail service for books both for the United States and abroad.

CHAPTER SIX

IMPORTANT FIGURES

IN PSYCHICAL RESEARCH

This chapter is devoted to brief biographical sketches of some of the major figures in the development and continuation of psychical research in various countries. It is by no means exhaustive, and only a few of the most significant facts about each person have been given. The aim is to enable the student to place the figure within the chronology of developments in the discipline and to have a ready reference for names he may encounter in his studies. For fuller treatment of these and other key people, the student should consult, for earlier ones only, Nandor Fodor's *Encyclopedia of Psychic Science*, University Books, New Hyde Park, New York, 1966, which is a reprint of the original 1933 edition, with some additions and corrections, and Helene Pleasants, Editor, *Biographical Dictionary of Parapsychology*, Helix Press, New York, 1964.

Arthur James Balfour, first Earl of Balfour, 1848-1930. Brother of Mrs. Eleanor Sidgwick and Gerald William Balfour, President of SPR, 1893. Prime Minister of Great Britain, 1902-05, and member of various governments in other capacities. While he took great interest in psychical research, outside of his Presidential Address to the SPR (*Proceedings,* Volume 10, Part 26, 1894), he did not contribute to the literature. The important "Palm Sunday Case" dealing with his belief that his sweetheart, Mary Lyttleton, who had died in 1875, had communicated, especially through "Mrs. Willett", was not published until 1960 (SPR *Proceedings,* Volume 52, Part 189). This is the most significant cross-correspondence of recent years.

Gerald William Balfour, second Earl of Balfour, 1853-1945. Brother of Mrs. Eleanor Sidgwick and Arthur James Balfour, President of SPR, 1906, 1907. Best known as a leading expert upon the cross-correspondences, in the investigation of which his deep classical erudition stood him in good stead, he came to accept survival and communication between discarnates and the living. His papers on the "Ear of Dionysius" case are major contributions to survival literature and one of the most exhaustive studies of cross-correspondence scripts. He was also much interested in the mechanics of mediumship and of the techniques used by purported discarnates to communicate.

Sir William F. Barrett, 1844-1925. Leader in the foundation of the Society for Psychical Research in 1882, and of the American Society for Psychical Research in 1885. Professor of Physics at the Royal College of Science, Dublin, 1873-1910. A leading physicist of his time, he was instrumental in establishing the high standards of evidence which have characterized the work of the SPR ever since. He wrote several books, including a large work on dowsing, which were widely read, and became convinced of survival.

John Beloff, Lecturer in Psychology, University of Edinburgh. A leader in experimental work in Great Britain, especially in attempts to learn whether subjects can be taught to improve their psi abilities. He has published numerous articles and book reviews in the *Journals* of both the British and the American SPR and in the *Journal of Parapsychology*. Author of *The Existence of Mind*, 1962.

Hans Bender, born 1907. Professor of Psychology, University of Freiburg, West Germany, Director of the Institute for the Study of Borderland Areas of Psychology and Mental Health, University of Freiburg since 1950. He has studied and written upon a wide variety of parapsychological topics and has translated some English works into German, but has been especially interested in poltergeist phenomena.

Lawrence J. Bendit, born 1898. A psychiatrist, Dr. Bendit received his M.D. Degree from Cambridge University with a thesis upon "Paranormal Cognition," the first such degree to be awarded. His special interests are the relationships of paranormal occurrences with psychiatric conditions and the development of psychic faculties. His wife, Phoebe Payne Bendit, was a gifted clairvoyant, and together they have written several books, most widely read of which are *The Psychic Sense* and *This World and That*.

Henri Bergson, 1859-1951. One of the major French philosophers of the twentieth century, Nobel Prize winner, President of the SPR, 1913. A leading dualist, Bergson saw a clear dichotomomy between the *élan vital*, the creative life force as expressed in thought, and matter. Consequently, the paranormal phenomena which suggested strongly this dualistic nature of existence fit into his scheme well. He was convinced of survival, since thought is in no way dependent upon the material brain, but utilizes the brain. His presidential address to the SPR (SPR *Proceedings*, Volume 27, 1914) delineates most clearly his views on psychical research.

Theodore Besterman, born 1904. Former research officer and librarian of the SPR, distinguished librarian and bibliographer. Although he has not been active in psychical research since the late 1930's, his contributions in the 1920's and early 1930's are important. He assisted Sir William Barrett in his work on the divining rod, and later wrote his own book on the same topic, investigated several leading European mediums and reported his findings in *Some Modern Mediums*, participated in the impressive tests with the Polish medium Ossowiecki, and in those of the physical medium, Rudi Schneider.

C. D. Broad, 1887-1971. Professor of Philosophy and Fellow of Trinity College, Cambridge University, President of the Society for Psychical Research, 1935, 1958-60. Professor Broad, one of the most distinguished academic figures of his time, published numerous studies of the philosophical and evidential problems connected with psi phenomena, especially mediumistic data, precognition, and the survival hypothesis. Especially important are his *Religion, Philosophy, and Psychical Research*, and *Lectures on Psychical Research*.

Sir Cyril Burt, 1883-1971. Professor of psychology,

emeritus, London University. Sir Cyril, regarded as the dean of British psychologists, specializing in the psychology of education and problem children's learning processes, pursued research into mediumship, telepathy among children, co-operated in some of Dr. Soal's telepathic experiments, and has wrote upon the relationship between psychical phenomena and psychology. His Myers Memorial Lecture for 1968, *Psychology and Psychical Research*, is one of the most important syntheses of the two disciplines in recent years.

W. Whately Carington, 1884-1947. British psychical research and writer, editor of *Psyche*, 1921-37, author of many articles and books upon various aspects of psychical research. Noted especially for the usc of "free materials" in telepathy tests, Carington discovered the "displacement effect" in these experiments, and suggested to S. G. Soal that he re-examine Soal's disappointing attempts to replicate J. B. Rhine's early card-guessing successful results. This led to Soal's important work with Shackleton and Mrs. Stewart. Carington also introduced the word-association tests with mediums, experimented with PK and postulated his telepathic theory of "psychons" associated in various patterns. His book *Telepathy: An Outline of Its Facts, Theory, and Implications* is a major contribution to the field.

Hereward Carrington, 1880-1958. Leading psychical researcher and author. A highly trained amateur magician and shrewd observer, Dr. Carrington specialized early in his career in exposing physical mediums, investigated Eusapia Palladino exhaustively, sat on the *Scientific American* committee which examined "Margery"'s mediumship, and wrote dozens of books, the most important of which deal with physical mediumship and phenomena.

Edgar Cayce, 1877-1945. American sensitive. Over a long period, while "asleep," in a dissociated state, he apparently could diagnose the illnesses of people not present and clairvoyantly prescribe treatment which the patients often claimed proved efficacious. The Association for Research and Enlightenment at Virginia Beach, Virginia, directed by his son, High Lynn Cayce, is devoted to the study of Edgar Cayce's work and teachings regarding health, reincarnation, the significance of dreams, and geological changes of a major kind he forecast during the last four decades of the twentieth century.

C. T. K. Chari, born 1909. Professor and Chairman of the Department of Philosophy and Psychology, Madras Christian College, India. Professor Chari has written articles concerning the mathematical, scientific, psychological, and philosophical problems and issues connected with psychical research in American, British, and Indian publications.

Florence Cook, 1856-1904. Controversial medium whose ostensible materializations of a full figure claiming to be "Katie King," were observed and supported by Sir William Crookes. Trevor Hall has argued that Crookes lied to maintain the secrecy of his affair with Florence Cook, and this has thrown into further doubt the veracity of the phenomena reported.

Winifred Coombe-Tennant, ("Mrs. Willett"), 1874-1956. One of the "SPR group" of mediums involved in the cross-correspondences, Mrs. Coombe-Tennant maintained her anonymity under the pseudonym of "Mrs. Willett." One of the most gifted automatists in the history of psychical research, a woman of great intellectual gifts, socially prominent, a delegate to the League of Nations, she co-operated with many investigators, especially Sir Oliver Lodge and Gerald Balfour, in the production of automatic writing as well as spoken material, referred to as "Daylight Impressions." The paranormal content of her material is considered impressive and is among the strongest evidentially for survival yet produced. Mrs. Coombe-Tennant became once again prominent in psychical research with the publication of *Swan on a Black Sea* in 1965, by Geraldine Cummins, which purports to be scripts dictated by the discarnate Mrs. Coombe-Tennant to the Irish automatist. This work Professor C.D. Broad considered the most important survival evidence produced for many years.

Mina Crandon, "Margery," died 1941. Physical and direct voice medium, wife of a member of the Harvard Medical School faculty, she claimed to be under the control of her deceased brother "Walter." The "Margery" case was probably the most controversial in the history of psychical research. Some investigators were convinced of the reality of paranormal phenomena, but a majority held that they were fraudulent. The latter view was greatly strengthened after the discovery of the striking similarity between a "materialized" thumbprint of "Walter" and that of Crandon's dentist. There is a large literature, with photographs, upon the case, which attracted the *Scientific American's* attention as well as that of Harry Houdini, in both the British and the American societies' publications.

Sir William Crookes, 1832-1919. President of the SPR, 1896-99, physicist and early pioneer in psychical research. One of the 19th century's greatest scientists, Crookes' investigations of D. D. Home's mediumship convinced him of the reality of his phenomena, and the publication of his findings led to strong attacks upon him in scientific circles. His lengthy experiments with Florence Cook and "Katie King," together with photographs taken by Crookes which purported to show the medium and the materialized "spirit" side by side aroused a tremendous controversy still unresolved. While in his later life, he undertook little research, he continued his interest in mediumship, became convinced of survival through sittings which gave evidential material purporting to come from his deceased wife, and said shortly before his death that he remained utterly certain of the reality of psychic phenomena and materialization.

Geraldine Cummins, d. 1970. Irish automatist, writer. One of the most important automatists of the century, she produced some remarkable scripts. Beginning in 1923 and continuing until her death, these scripts included some purporting to originate from Frederic Myers, brought together in *The Road to Immortality*, and a long series, *The Scripts of Cleophas*, which deal with Biblical times and which some distinguished Biblical scholars pronounced as accurate and shedding light upon puzzling aspects of the New Testament. Her final work of great moment was *Swan on a Black Sea*, 1965 (new edition, 1970), consisting of scripts purportedly from "Mrs. Willett" or Mrs. Coombe-Tennant, the famous cross-correspondence automatist, which C. D. Broad considered the most important survival evidence produced for many years, but which was criticized in some quarters.

E. Douglas Dean, born 1916. Chemist, parapsychologist.

While he has conducted experiments dealing with PK, dowsing, homing pigeons, and other facets of psi, possibly his most significant work has been done with the plethysmograph. This instrument records changes in blood supply to a part of the body, such as a finger or ear lobe, depending upon the emotional response to a mental stimulus. With this, Dean has experimented on volunteers to determine if telepathy or clairvoyance can be detected under laboratory conditions between agent and subject. His results have been encouraging, and have led to other attempts at instrumentalization of experiments in parapsychology.

Eric J. Dingwall. Psychical researcher, anthropologist, author, librarian. Formerly research officer for the Society for Psychical Research, his knowledge of psychical research's development and the vast literature connected with its history is probably unrivalled. A highly critical and astute investigator, he has been involved in many of the most significant cases, such as that of Ossowiecki, "Eva C.," "Margery," Rudi and Willi Schneider, and re-examination of the Borley Rectory haunting reported by Harry Price.

E. R. Dodds, born 1893, Professor of Greek, emeritus, Oxford University, President of the SPR, 1961-62. Professor Dodds has been especially interested in the paranormal among ancient peoples and has written several excellent treatises upon this topic. Doubtless his most significant contribution to psychical research, however, is his most perceptive and cogent article, "Why I Do Not Believe in Survival," *Proceedings,* Volume XLII: 147-72, 1934. This summarizes in a brilliant manner the objections to the spiritist hypothesis, while taking full notice of mediumistic evidence, by emphasizing the alternative explanations.

Mrs. John H. Curran, died 1936. The sensitive through whom the works of "Patience Worth" were produced. Beginning with the ouija board in 1913, for over twenty years Mrs. Curran wrote automatically and dictated poems, epigrams, and several novels pronounced remarkable literary works by experts, with uncanny accuracy of knowledge about Biblical and medieval times, and very unusual philological consistency in keeping with the insistence of "Patience Worth" that she was the spirit of a woman who had lived in the mid-seventeenth century. Walter Franklin Prince made an exhaustive ten month study of Mrs. Curran, and published his results in 1927, in one of the principal works of psychical research, *The Case of Patience Worth.*

Hans Driesch, 1867-1941. Philosopher and embryologist, President of the SPR, 1926-27. He espoused the philosophy of "vitalism" which held that cells have an innate characteristic of purposefully struggling for the development of the entire organism of which it is a part; hence, he rejected the blind determinism of current materialism. He co-operated with researchers in Britain, America, and Europe and participated in investigations of some of the outstanding physical and mental mediums of the period such as the Schneider brothers and Mrs. Leonard. He was doubtful about physical phenomena, but was more impressed with telepathy, precognition, and clairvoyance.

C. J. Ducasse, 1881-1969. Philosopher, Professor of Philosophy at Brown University. One of America's most esteemed philosophers, Dr. Ducasse was noted for the lucidity of his thought and writing. While he concerned himself with all aspects of psychical research, his greatest interests were in precognition, mediumship, survival, and the construction of an undergirding theoretical framework for psi. His articles on survival and his book, *A Critical Examination of the Belief in a Life After Death* are vital contributions to the study of the survival problem.

J. W. Dunne, 1875-1949. Aeronautical engineer, writer. Dunne is best known for his book, *An Experiement with Time*, in which he described his numerous precognitive dreams and postulated a concept of "serialism." This theory held that there is an infinite regression of Times, each observed by a different facet of the personality, so that Time is a dimension with an infinite number of subdivisions within it. His views have not won acceptance and have been sharply criticized by many philosophers and scientists, but the precognitive aspects of his works remain most arresting.

Simeon Edmunds, born 1917. Former research secretary of the College of Psychic Science (now Studies) in London, psychical researcher, writer, hypnotist. A highly critical student of paranormal phenomena, his study of "spirit photography" published by the Society for Psychical Research dismisses as fraudulent all such claims, while his study of spiritualism, *Spiritualism: A Critical Survey*, is a strong attack upon the movement's credulity, widespread fraud, and self-delusion.

Harry Edwards, born 1893. Spiritual healer. Probably the most famous of such healers, Edwards believes that the healing which he claims takes place, and to which letters from patients attest, is performed by discarnates working through him, rather than by means of any healing power he possesses himself. Medical authorities have remained highly dubious of Edwards' statistics and of the attestation of patients, although some doctors have indicated interest in healing. Of recent years, there has been considerable increase in medical attention to spiritual healing, although medical figures tend to attribute improvement to psychosomatic causes and not to discarnate or other paranormal sources.

F. H. Everard Feilding, 1867-1936. Barrister, psychical researcher, secretary of the SPR, 1903-1920. An exceedingly acute investigator whose articles demonstrated his care of detail, control in experiments, and painstaking thoroughness, Feilding's most significant contribution is his study, with Hereward Carrington and William Baggally, of Eusapia Palladino in 1908, which remains a classic in psychical research, and which convinced him of the reality of physical phenomena.

Camille Flammarion, 1842-1925. Astronomer; President of the SPR, 1923. A very distinguished astronomer, Flammarion early in his career became involved in paranormal investigations and in spiritualism through reading Allan Kardec's works. He attended a great many seances of both mental and physical mediums, invited Eusapia Palladino to Paris for experiments, and after fifty years, became convinced of survival, the reality of hauntings, physical phenomena, and virtually the entire range of psychic occurrences. His most widely read work is his three volume treatise *Death and Its Mysteries.*

Alice Kipling Fleming, "Mrs. Holland," 1868-1948. Automatist; sister of Rudyard Kipling, longtime resident of India. While Mrs. Fleming had had some success with automatic writing for her own amusement, she became seriously interested following her reading of Myers's *Human Personality and Its Survival of Bodily Death*, and this led to her participation as a member of the "SPR group" in the cross-correspondences during the first decade of this century. Messages purportedly from Myers, Gurney, and Sidgwick were produced and some were found to correspond strikingly with other scripts ostensibly from the same sources obtained by other automatists in Britain and America with whom Mrs. Fleming had no contact.

Antony G. N. Flew, born 1923. Philosopher. Professor of Philosophy at Keele University. Professor Flew is concerned principally with the precise use of language, measurement, and concepts in psychical research. He has been highly critical of much of the work, both qualitative and quantitative, produced and of the philosophical deductions based upon that work. A humanist and atheist, he feels that only the statistical evidence of repeatable experiments can firmly establish psi phenomena, and that while sufficient evidence for psi has already been gathered to warrant utilizing its existence as a hypothesis, there is nothing in such phenomena to warrant religious, survivalistic, or dualistic constructions. His book, *A New Approach to Psychical Research* discusses his views.

Theodore Flournoy, 1854-1920. Psychologist. Dr. Flournoy was an eminent Swiss psychologist, friend of William James, and best known for his important study of Hélène Smith in *From India to the Planet Mars.* From his lengthy and exhaustive research upon the ostensible discarnate control "Leopold" and the medium's two former "incarnations," Marie Antoinette and an Indian princess, Flournoy concluded that the language of "Mars" was an intricate subconscious construction upon French roots, that "Marie Antoinette" was a subconscious dramatization, but that the veridical information about the Hindu princess was truly paranormal, although not of a discarnate source.

Having also investigated Eusapia Palladino, surveyed apparitions and hauntings, Flournoy was convinced of PK, telepathy, clairvoyance, and possible survival, although he doubted that communication with the dead took place. *From India to the Planet Mars* remains one of the most extraordinary studies in the annals of psychical research.

Nandor Fodor, 1895-1964. Psychical researcher, psychologist, writer. Fodor was especially interested in the relationship between psychoanalysis and the paranormal. In his varied career, Fodor changed his views on spiritualism, beginning as rather credulous, swinging to highly critical, and in his later years veering towards a mid-point. He had a wide experience with all types of mediums, engaged in highly publicized feuds, and was a very colorful and knowledgeable man. His *Encyclopedia of Psychic Science,* first published in 1933, shows an astonishing knowledge of the field together with his youthful tendency to editorialize his own views. His later books were more sober and gave some perceptive insights into the possible connections between psychological disturbances, analysis, and psi faculties and manifestations.

Haakon Gabriel Forwald, born 1897. Electrical engineer, inventor. Forwald has concerned himself for over twenty years with experiments upon PK. He has pursued this interest not only in his native Sweden, but in America as well. Convinced that he has demonstrated statistically the reality of PK, he has postulated a theory to account for the direction and final placement of the dice used in the experiments. He has probably undertaken more experiments in PK research than any other investigator; the principal criticism directed towards his work by other parapsychologists is that most of it has been conducted by Forwald alone, thus robbing it of verifiability by witnesses.

Eileen J. Garrett (1893-1970). Medium, writer, editor. One of the major trance mediums of the century, Mrs. Garrett also was highly gifted as a writer, businesswoman, administrator, and editor. She retained an unusually critical viewpoint about her own mediumship, and was eager to co-operate in any scientific investigations which would throw light upon mediumship and all other types of psi faculties and phenomena. To this end, she was involved in many experiments with leading psychical researchers in Great Britain, America, and Europe; and she founded the Parapsychology Foundation in 1951 to further research through financial grants, conferences, and publications. She was a prolific writer with perceptive views and rewarding insights into life which her varied experiences had provided. Her three autobiographical works are especially important: *My Life in Search for the Meaning of Mediumship, 1938; Adventures in the Supernormal, 1943;* and *Many Voices, 1968.*

Gustave Geley, 1868-1924. Psychical Researcher, physician, Director of the Institut Métapsychique International, 1919-24. Geley was a leading student of physical phenomena. He participated in investigations of Eva C., and obtained the famous plaster casts produced by the Polish medium Kluski which pointed to materialization under laboratory conditions. He co-operated in much of his research with the distinguished French physiologist Charles Richet. The most significant work Geley wrote is *From the Unconscious to the Conscious,* one of the principal books produced by European psychical research.

Kathleen M. H. Goldney, psychical researcher, Council

member, SPR, 1943-present, Organizing Secretary, SPR, 1949-57. Mrs. Goldney has long been a prominent and highly respected figure in British research. She has studied mediumship extensively and written about the work of Mrs. Hughes and Mrs. Garrett; she collaborated in the famous Shackleton tests with Dr. Soal; she was involved in the Borley Rectory case both with Harry Price and since his death, for she was joint author, with Dr. Dingwall and Mr. Hall, of the critical study of Price's investigation of Borley, *The Haunting of Borley Rectory,* in which doubt is cast upon a sizeable part of Price's evidence and conclusions.

Edmund Gurney, 1847-1888. Psychical researcher, psychologist. One of the Trinity College, Cambridge group, he was a founder of the Society for Psychical Research. An indefatigable investigator, with a brilliant mind, deep knowledge of many fields including hypnotism, in which he was an acknowledged authority, Gurney did as much as anyone to establish the high standards of evidentiality, thorough scrutiny of cases, and distinguished level of literary style which have characterized the best work of the SPR. He collaborated with Frederic Myers in the classic work, *Phantasms of the Living, 1886,* which remains an essential book in psychical research.

C. E. M. Hansel, born 1917. Psychologist. Possibly the most voiciferous and prolific critic of contemporary parapsychology, Professor Hansel has published several articles analyzing statistical experiments which have been cited by leading investigators as establishing psi as a reality, and has found major flaws in all such results and claims. His major work is *ESP: A Scientific Evaluation, 1966,* in which he argues that ESP is highly unlikely, has not been verified by the canons of scientific evidentialty due to the absence of a truly repeatable experiment, and can be explained by the hypothesis of trickery on the part of subjects or psychical researchers or both. This latter hypothesis he proposes as the most likely answer. The book has been vigorously attacked by parasychologists in many countries.

Sir Alister C. Hardy, born 1896. Zoologist, Professor of Zoology emeritus, Oxford University; President of the SPR, 1965-69. A distinguished scientist, Fellow of the Royal Society, renowned expert upon oceanography, Sir Alister founded the Religious Experience Research Unit at Oxford upon his retirement. There he and his staff are undertaking the collection of accounts of religious experiences and analysis of the common denominators to be found in various types of such accounts. He has been especially concerned with the revolutionary implications of psychical research for theories of biology, religion, and philosophy. He has brought together his views regarding these matters in two major works, the product of his Gifford Lectures, *The Living Stream, 1965* and *The Divine Flame*, 1966.

Hornell Hart, 1888-1967. Sociologist, psychical researcher. Dr. Hart was a member of the faculty at Duke University for almost twenty years, and during that period he became involved in psi research, and continued his work after leaving Duke. Especially interested in apparitions and a leading scholar upon this subject—his article, "Six Theories About Apparitions" in the *SPR Journal*, May, 1956, is a very important contribution—he was also concerned with out-of-the-body experiences, and the survival issue. His book, *The*

Enigma of Survival: The Case For and Against an Afterlife, 1959, is a significant addition to the literature.

Renée Haynes (Mrs. Jerrard Tickell), born 1906. Writer, psychical researcher, editor of *The Journal* of the SPR. Miss Haynes has long been interested in the paranormal and has been involved in numerous investigations as well as contributing to the *SPR Journal* before assuming her current position as Editor. She is the author of several books, including a very original treatment of psi, *The Hidden Springs*, and a biographical study of the 18th century Pope Benedict XIV, who evinced interest in the paranormal, *The Philosopher Pope, 1971*

Rosalind Heywood, born 1895. Psychical researcher, writer, sensitive. Mrs. Heywood, for many years a member of the Council of the Society for Psychical Research, is a leading figure in psychical research in Great Britain. She combines a natural sensitivity to psi with a rare critical acumen and literary gift for elucidating the evidence and significance of psi for the layman. Her experimental work as a subject and her study as an investigator have placed her in an unusually sound position to judge both the subjective and the objective aspects of research. Her two books, *The Sixth Sense* (*Beyond the Reach of Sense*, American title), 1959; and her autobiographical study, *The Infinite Hive* (*ESP: A Personal Memoir*, American title), 1964, are among the finest general treatments of psi yet produced.

Richard Hodgson, 1855-1905. Psychical researcher official of the American Society for Psychical Research, 1887-1905. A brilliant Australian psychologist who came under the influence of Henry Sidgwick at Cambridge, Hodgson became a leader in the SPR at its inception, and was sent to India to investigate the claims of Madame Blavatsky and her Theosophical Society. His report was strongly critical, accusing Madame Blavatsky and others of fraudulent phenomena. Highly skeptical, he demonstrated the role of conjuring in producing ostensible psychic phenomena, showed the low observational skills of participants in seances, and was interested in secondary personalities. When William James was impressed with Mrs. Piper's mediumship, Hodgson came to Boston to investigate her with a strong predilection that she was fraudulent. After the most stringent precautions, over a period of years, he became convinced not only of her psi faculty but of the discarnate source for much of her information. His conversion to the survivalist position appreciably strengthened that school of thought in the early stages of psychical research due to the high regard in which he was held. He contributed many articles to the *SPR Proceedings* and helped edit Myers's monumental study for publication after Myers's death.

Daniel Dunglas Home, 1833-1886. Medium. The most famous of physical mediums, Home produced a wide range of phenomena including levitation, partial materialization, psychokinetic effects, bodily elongation, and imperviousness to fire, all generally demonstrated in full light in contrast to virtually every other physical medium's requirement for darkness. He was a celebrity, entertained by the royalty of European courts, lavished with gifts (he never accepted fees for his demonstrations), investigated by such distinguished scientists as Crookes in Great Britain and Hare in America, and he convinced many outstanding figures of the reality of his phenomena. Despite numerous attempts to discover fraud in his mediumship, Home is probably alone among principal physical mediums in never having been found using trickery or devices. Those who remained skeptical of his gift claimed mass hypnosis as the explanation for the conviction of witnesses. While there were some unsavory, or at best, unpleasant, aspects to his personal life, including expulsion from Rome as a wizard and a highly publicized trial over money, his mediumship remains the most impressive instance of physical phenomena on record.

William James, 1842-1910. Psychologist, philosopher, psychical researcher. Professor of Philosophy and of Psychology at Harvard University, founder of the American Society for Psychical Research; President of the SPR, 1894-95. One of the most famous and influential figures of his day, James was a pioneer in the infant discipline of psychology, formulated his pragmatic philosophy, contributed to the study of religion with his classic *The Varieties of Religious Experience*, became a chief protagonist of psychical research, and discovered one of the most important of mediums, Mrs. Piper, co-operating in her investigation with Richard Hodgson. He became convinced of the reality of the psi faculty and announced that both mental and physical phenomena, surrounded though the true were with the fraudulent, should be studied in the same spirit and with the same thoroughness as other natural phenomena. His enormous prestige greatly strengthened psychical research and encouraged other scholars to consider it a field worthy of research. His writings upon psychical research have been edited and collected in the volume *William James on Psychical Research*, 1960.

Carl J. Jung, 1875-1961. Psychiatrist. Jung became interested in paranormal phenomena as a young man, investigated mediums, co-operated with the great German psychical researcher Schrenk-Notzing, lectured before the SPR in 1919, formulated his concept of "synchronicity" as a possible explanation of the baffling acausal relationships found in psi phenomena, and urged other psychiatrists and psychologists to consider parapsychology as an essential aspect of their discipline. His knowledge of the occult was considerable as well, and he insisted, in the face of hostile critics, that whatever the source and validity of occult theories and practices and of paranormal phenomena, the fact that many people held such theories and believed in the reality of such phenomena meant that psychologists must investigate them.

G. W. Lambert, retired civil servant, President of the SPR, 1955-58, former Hon. Secretary of the SPR. Mr. Lambert has proven to be an indefatigable, painstaking, and thorough researcher, especially with regard to alternative theories to paranormal causation in reported instances of ostensible psi phenomena. His study of poltergeist cases and the bearing of possible physical factors often overlooked is a major contribution. He has collaborated recently with Mr. MacKenzie in his collection of cases, and has studied intensively personal references in the cross-correspondence material, especially that of Mrs. Verrall. He has also written important analyses of the famous Versailles "Adventure" and the "Dieppe air raid case".

Gladys Osborne Leonard, 1882-1970. Medium. One of the greatest of trance mediums, Mrs. Leonard was exhaustively investigated over a long period by the leading psychical researchers of Great Britain. She participated in the "book tests" and "newspaper tests," especially with Rev. Drayton Thomas, and was one of the principal subjects for Whately Carington's Word Association Tests to determine whether her control, "Feda" was a secondary personality or an ostensible discarnate. Made famous by Sir Oliver Lodge's book *Raymond* in which he recounted his conviction that he had communicated with his dead son through her mediumship, Mrs. Leonard for some time accepted sitters exclusively through the SPR, and many were convinced of survival by evidential material received. Unlike Mrs. Garrett, Mrs. Leonard was a spiritualist, and utterly sure of survival; but this personal conviction did not deter her from co-operating in every controlled experiment proposed by researchers. Her personal and professional integrity were above reproach and she remains an extraordinary example of remarkable psi abilities and tireless willingness to investigate. Her most significant book is *My Life in Two Worlds*, 1931.

Sir Oliver J. Lodge, 1851-1940. Physicist, educator, psychical researcher; President of the SPR, 1901-03, 1932. A distinguished physicist, renowned for his research into electricity and radio among other scientific projects, Lodge pursued investigations into psi from the mid 1880's. He studied the mediumship of Mrs. Piper and Mrs. Leonard exhaustively, participated in the cross-correspondences, led in the "book tests" and the development of "proxy sittings" to help eliminate telepathy from the sitter as alternative explanations to discarnate sources for veridical data. At length convinced of survival, he wrote voluminously, and created a sensation with his work *Raymond*, 1916, in which he detailed why he was convinced of the survival of his son killed in World War I, through the mediumship especially of Mrs. Leonard and Vout Peters. He devised a posthumous test to try and demonstrate his own survival; and while the test itself has been assessed quite differently as to its success, it has led to other more sophisiticated ideas in such tests.

William McDougall, 1871-1938. Psychologist, psychical researcher. McDougall was an eminent dualist psychologist and philosopher whose interest in psychical research was aroused by the work of William James at Harvard. When McDougall became Professor of Psychology at Harvard, he urged that psychical research be accepted as a regular discipline of study. His opportunity to put this concept into action came when he was invited to chair the department of psychology at Duke University and from this came the Parapsychology Laboratory headed by Dr. J.B. Rhine. McDougall's international eminence as a psychologist and philosopher made his support for psychical research especially useful.

William Stainton Moses, 1839-1892. Medium, clergyman. Best known as one of the earliest practitioners of automatic writing, there was some evidence of physical phenomena in the earlier stages of his mediumship, but these had apparently subsided by the time Moses participated in the founding of the SPR in 1882. Convinced of survival and of the discarnate source for evidential material as well as the religious teachings in his automatic writing, Moses resigned from the SPR because he felt its leaders were unfairly critical of spiritualism. His best known work is *Spirit Teachings*, 1883.

Gardner Murphy, born 1895. Psychologist, psychical researcher; President of the SPR, 1949; President of the

ASPR, 1962-1971. An eminent psychologist, Dr. Murphy studied at Harvard when McDougall was there, and has been interested in psi throughout his career. His numerous articles have reflected his wide concerns with both the experimental and the theoretical aspects of parapsychology, for he has written about telepathy, clairvoyance, precognition, survival, the body-mind issue, mediumship, and the bearing psychical research has upon religious views. He is greatly concerned that a repeatable experiment be developed, for this, he feels, is essential if psi phenomena and their investigation are to become an integral part of psychology in general as he thinks they should. His general work on psychical research, *The Challenge of Psychical Research,* 1961, is one of the finest overall treatments of the disipline.

Gilbert Murray, 1866-1957. Professor of Greek, Oxford University; President of the SPR, 1915-16, 1952. Murray was one of the foremost classical scholars of his generation and moved in a distinguished academic community, some of whom were more than surprised at his interest in psychical research. His chief contribution to the field lies in the reports of his own remarkable telepathic abilities. The demonstration of this gift took the form of Murray leaving the room while a group of his family and friends decided upon a scene or idea for him to discover. He then was recalled, held the hand of the person with the concept, and in an unusually high percentage of instances guessed the precise scene or idea. Some critics have credited Murray with a "telaesthesia" or greatly heightened hearing and sensing ability rather than telepathy, so that he physically heard the discussion despite his distance from the room. The participants in the tests, however, have discounted this due to the nature of the building and its heavy walls. The Murray tests, while not easily quantifiable, are probably the most impressive qualitative demonstrations of telepathy on record.

Frederic W. H. Myers, 1843-1901. Poet, classicist, psychical researcher, founder of the SPR; President of the SPR, 1900. His interest in psychical research sprang from two roots: first, his close friendship and great admiration for Henry Sidgwick; second, his intense desi ɔ to prove for himself and for all the reality of survival. During the twenty years between the founding of the SPR and his death, Myers devoted most of his time and energy and a considerable sum of money to the investigation, publication, and publicizing of psychical phenomena. Although a classicist by training and a poet by inclination, he steeped himself in the rudimentary psychology of his day, and based upon that and his own deep knowledge of the evidence so far gathered for psi, he postulated bold theories, insisted upon high standards for the new discipline, and laid the foundation for what has ensured. Probably more than any other, Myers could be called the founder of psychical research. His perceptive ideas in the classic *Phantasms of the Living* which he prepared with Gurney and Podmore in 1886, plus his many articles in the *SPR Proceedings*; and especially the extraordinary insights of the most important single work in the literature of psychical research, the mammoth *Human Personality and Its Survival of Bodily Death:* these contributions are unexcelled.

Eugene Osty, 1874-1938. Physician, psychical researcher, Director of the Institut Métapsychique International in Paris. Osty worked closely in his psychical studies with Charles Richet, Gustave Geley, Henri Bergson, and

Emile Boirac. His critical acumen, insistence upon careful experimental controls, lucid writing, and thorough investigation were all outstanding. While especially interested in mental phenomena, he did become convinced of the reality of PK through investigation of Rudi Schneider. Like Richet, he rejected the spiritualist hypothesis and argued that psi phenomena and faculties were other aspects of human nature that must be studied in the same dispassionate, scientific manner as the physiological factors. Like many researchers of his generation, he was overly optimistic as to the early establishment of the reality of psi among the orthodox scientists; but he repeatedly challenged them to investigate the evidence, repeat the experiments, and see for themselves. Besides the vast numbers of articles he wrote, probably his most significant work is *Supernormal Faculties in Man*, 1925.

Eusapia Palladino, 1854-1918. Medium. Possibly the greatest physical medium since Home, or possibly the cleverest of fraudulent mediums, Palladino was certainly the most controversial of her time. No other medium except "Margery" has so divided the psychical researchers in their assessments. Studied by virtually every important investigator in Europe, Great Britain, and America during her career, she undoubtedly cheated when she could or needed to; but many shrewd experts were convinced of the reality of her phenomena under stringent conditions. These phenomena, ostensibly under the direction of her control "John King," included levitation of Eusapia herself, of tables, chairs, tambourines, trumpets, strange flitting lights, the playing of a small guitar, raps, etc. The distinguished investigator, Hereward Carrington, possibly was closest to the truth when he held that Eusapia, a highly erotic, mischievous, impatient woman, enjoyed fooling investigators, was uninterested in proving her gift, and cheated when she could not or would not produce real phenomena. The most thorough investigation of Eusapia Palladino's mediumship is in the volume by Feilding, Carrington, and Baggally dealing with their series of sittings in 1908, *Sittings with Eusapia Palladino and Other Studies.*

Leonore E. S. Piper, 1859-1950. Medium. Mrs. Piper was "discovered" by William James in Boston, where she was a member of a socially prominent family. Sure that she did indeed have a paranormal gift, he arranged for Richard Hodgson to come from England to investigate her; Hodgson was at length not only certain of her psi faculty, but became convinced of survival through her mediumship. For thirty years, Mrs. Piper was investigated thoroughly by the most prominent and careful of American and British researchers, and all attested to her utter integrity, constant co-operation despite the considerable inconveniences caused by the stringent precautions imposed, and the remarkably consistent quality of her gift. Her trance work was both oral and through automatic writing. She participated in the cross-correspondences, in which the material of a recondite classical nature completely foreign to her own limited knowledge is especially impressive. There are numerous articles dealing with her mediumship in the publications of both the ASPR and the SPR, and her daughter, Alta, has written a sympathetic and perceptive brief biography, *The Life and Work of Mrs. Piper,* 1929.

Frank Podmore, 1856-1910. Psychical researcher,

government official. Podmore was early in his life converted to spiritualism; but the widespread fraud among mediums severely disillusioned him and he swung to the highly critical point on the spectrum, a position he retained for many years. His massive study, *Modern Spiritualism*, 1902, is sharply critical of the entire movement but it is thoroughly researched and remains a principal volume in the literature. He collaborated with Myers and Gurney in the preparation of *Phantasms of the Living*, 1886, investigated many cases of ostensible poltergeist and apparition phenomena, studied Mrs. Piper, postulated a variation of the hallucinatory theory of apparitions, and followed the cross-correspondences closely. The high evidentiality of the latter caused him shortly before his death to indicate that his anti-spiritualistic hypothesis position was changing. He was one of the most thorough and skeptical of the early researchers and his contributions to the discipline are manifold.

J. Gaither Pratt, born 1910. Parapsychologist. A world-renowned experimental parapsychologist, Dr. Pratt worked with Dr. J.B. Rhine at Duke University for thirty years before joining the staff at the Parapsychology Unit of the University of Virginia. His tests with Pearce and Woodruff are considered, together with Dr. Soal's experiments with Shackleton and Mrs. Stewart, the most impressive statistical evidence for ESP yet produced. Recently he has conducted extensive tests with the Czech sensitive, Pavel Stepanek, on the "focussing effect"; continued the investigation of the "thoughtography" of Ted Serios begun by Dr. Eisenbud; has also studied the possibly paranormal faculties of homing pigeons, the Seaforth poltergeist case; and has developed, with Birge, a method for quantifying qualitative material for statistical analysis and assessment. He has collaborated on several works with J. B. Rhine, and wrote his own account, *Parapsychology: An Insider's View of ESP,* 1966.

Harry Price, 1881-1948. Psychical researcher, writer. A rather flamboyant and controversial figure in his lifetime, Price has continued to arouse dispute posthumously over his most famous case, the "haunting" of Borley Rectory. A study of the case by Eric Dingwall, K. M. Goldney, and Trevor Hall published by the SPR argued that Price himself had fraudulently produced some of the most striking phenomena through his excellent legerdemain (he was an outstanding amateur magician). Recently Robert J. Hastings has written a refutation of those charges, and the controversy continues. Price established his own investigative organization, the National Laboratory of Psychical Research, in London, developed an enormous personal library of about 15,000 volumes dealing with magic, the occult, and psychical research which he left to the University of London, wrote hundreds of articles and many books of a popular nature, and investigated many mediums including Rudi Schneider, Helen Duncan, Frau Silbert, Eleanore Zugun, Stella C., and Eileen Garrett. His apparent interest in publicity and the popular nature of his writings set him at odds with the scholarly pursuits of the SPR and other scientific bodies, but he did arouse public interest in psi phenomena and did point out the fraudulent practices of some mediums. One's assessment of Price remains a matter of personal predilection.

H. H. Price, born 1899. Professor of Logic, emeritus, Oxford University, President of the SPR, 1960-61. An exceedingly distinguished academic philosopher,

Professor Price has concerned himself principally with telepathy, mediumship, and the survival issue. Regarding the latter, he has written several articles postulating possible forms survival could conceivably take, and has argued that a "bodiless" survival is really unthinkable due to our need for personal identity, social acceptance, and love—all of which are premised upon some type of "bodily" recognition. Consequently, he has suggested that the tradition of an "astral" or "etheric" body may be a productive line of thought. He has also dealt with the problem of precognition, the mind-body issue, and other philosophical implications of psi.

Walter Franklin Prince, 1863-1934. Psychical researcher, minister, psychologist; President of the SPR, 1930-31. The ablest and most experienced American researcher of his day, Dr. Prince combined his knowledge of psychology, religion, and psychical research with a highly developed critical ability, natural shrewdness, and thorough scrutiny of every aspect of a case. His study of "Doris Fischer's" multiple personality is a classic of abnormal psychology, while his large volume, *The Case of Patience Worth*, 1927, is a major contribution to mediumistic literature. He remained highly skeptical of PK and other physical phenomena, but felt that there was no doubt at all of telepathy, clairvoyance and precognition. He pointed out the inherent difficulties of proving survival, but held that the best evidence, such as the cross-correspondences and the Chaffin will case, made the alternative hypotheses tenuous; consequently, while he believed in survival, he felt that psychical research had not established it empirically, nor was he sure it could. This realistic appraisal of the problems involved was unusual at that period and demonstrates the remarkable qualities Dr. Prince brought to the discipline.

J. B. Rhine, born 1895. Parapsychologist. Possibly the most widely known of all parapsychologists, no one has had a greater influence upon research during the last forty years. Following the establishment of the Parapsychology Laboratory under his direction, with the encouragement of William McDougall, at Duke University, Rhine undertook to devise repeatable and statistically measureable experiments. His early successes aroused a storm of controversy, and easy and frequent replication proved less likely than had been supposed; but Soal vindicated Rhine's findings impressively after initial failure, and other statistical studies have followed by the dozens. After the mathematics, randomness, laboratory controls, record-keeping, and possible sensory clues had all been investigated, some flaws corrected, and the general conclusions verified, the final and unanswerable criticism has been made by Hansel: collusion, involuntary and voluntary fraud among both subjects and investigators as the most likely hypothesis to cover the extrachance results, since ESP is intrinsically impossible. Dr. Rhine has joined other parapsychologists in replying vigorously to this and other attacks upon the scientific integrity of investigators. His numerous books, some scholarly, others directed to the general public, have made ESP a household term. The statistical evidence for psychokinesis has also been gathered by Rhine's co-workers, but this has met with less acceptance among other parapsychologists. Investigation of psi in animals, psychological traits and conditions conducive to and inhibitory of psi, their effects upon psi, and other topics have been undertaken, while the collection of spontaneous cases has proceeded under the direction of his wife, Dr. Louisa Rhine. After his retirement from Duke University, Dr. Rhine formed the Foundation for Reserch on the Nature of Man where he continues his research and supports other approaches to parapsychological investigations.

Charles Richet, 1850-1935. Physiologist, psychical researcher; President of the SPR, 1905. An outstanding physiologist, winner of the Nobel Prize in 1913, Richet was a cautious, careful, skeptical investigator who had strongly criticized William Crookes' acceptance of paranormal phenomena in the 1870's. However, he undertook his own studies and became a leading figure in European psychical research. Especially interested in physical phenomena, he studied Eusapia Palladino, Eva C., Kluski, Rudi Schneider, and other important mediums, coined the term "ectoplasm" for the quasi-physical substance supposedly used in materializations; with Geley, he obtained what he considered fraud-proof evidence for the reality of ectoplasmic phenomena under laboratory conditions; he wrote extensively about telepathy and precognition—particularly premonitory cases—and held firmly to an anti-spiritualistic interpretation of paranormal phenomena. Like Osty and other experts, he challenged scientists to experiment and investigate with an open mind and discover the reality of psi for themselves. His most important work is probably *Thirty Years of Psychical Research*, 1923.

W. H. Salter, 1880-1970. Barrister, psychical researcher; President of the SPR, 1947-48. Mr. Salter served the SPR in a variety of capacities over forty years and came to know all the key figures in psychical research in Great Britain and most of the nonBritish investigators as well. He was an excellent researcher, expert in dissecting testimony, postulating alternative explanations, and elucidating the issues in an unusually clear and judicious manner. Together with Piddington, Alice Johnson, and Gerald Balfour, Salter was a principal expert upon the cross-correspondences, his interest in these important cases being strong since his wife was Helen Verrall, whose mother was one of the "SPR group" of automatists and who also was an automatist, while her father was a member of the "Myers group" of ostensible discarnate communicators. In addition to his involvement with the survival issue, Salter studied apparitions thoroughly and wrote an excellent treatment of the subject, *Ghosts and Apparitions*, 1938. His last and largest book, *Zoar*, 1961, is one of the most important studies of survival yet produced.

H. F. Saltmarsh, 1881-1943. Psychical researcher, businessman. Saltmarsh was an important contributor to SPR work during the 1930's. He was among the earliest to attempt a quantifying method for qualitative material; he made a thorough study of the cross-correspondences, and his book, *Evidence of Personal Survival from Cross Correspondences*, 1938, remains the best brief introduction to that complex mass of data. He also wrote a clear account of the evidence for precognition and the various frustrating attempts to explain it in *Foreknowledge*, 1938.

Gertrude R. Schmeidler, born 1912. Psychologist, parapsychologist. Best known for her "sheep and goat" experiments in which she demonstrated that belief or disbelief in psi tends to affect the subject's psi performance so that it is congruent with his predilection, Dr. Schmeidler has also studied how various psychological conditions and patterns affect psi, the inter-relationship of the experimenter-subject rapport and successful results, and other laboratory-oriented projects. The book she wrote with Dr. McConnell, *ESP and Personality Patterns*, 1958, brought together many of the results of her research. She has also written many articles for the *ASPR Journal*.

Rudi Schneider, 1908-1957. Medium. A prominent physical medium in the 1920's and early 1930's, Rudi and his older brother Willy were investigated by leading researchers such as Schrenk-Notzing, who discovered them in Austria, Richet, Osty, various SPR researchers, and Harry Price. Very stringent conditions were generally imposed including a complete physical examination, sewing into a one piece suit with luminous markings which showed in the dark, sitting in a cage, infra-red photography, etc. Rudi's phenomena included the apparent psychokinetic movement of small objects such as a trumpet, bell, doll, strumming a zither, and the ectoplasmic materialization of a three-fingered hand. While Price and others said that Rudi had on occasion cheated when the conditions were lax, a large number of investigators were convinced that truly paranormal phenomena were produced under fraud-proof conditions.

Albert von Schrenk-Notzing, 1862-1929. Physician, psychical researcher. His medical training led to his interest in hypnotism and thence to psychical research, an interest which was encouraged through his friendship with Charles Richet. Schrenk-Notzing studied many aspects of psi, but was best known for his forty years of work on physical phenomena, in which he cooperated with Osty, Geley, Lodge, and earlier figures such as Myers. He devised many of the precautionary procedures which were widely adopted such as the complete physical examinations, one-piece luminous suits, and dyes in fluids to detect if ectoplasmic material had been regurgitated fraudulently. He investigated major physical mediums such as Eva C., Eusapia Palladino, Tomcyzk, and the Schneider brothers; and he became convinced, as did Osty, Richet, Geley, and some others, that materializations did occur under fraud-proof conditions. He translated some non-German works into his own language, established his own laboratory, and wrote numerous articles and books, principally upon physical phenomena. It is interesting to note that like most European researchers who accepted the reality of the controversial physical phenomena, he rejected the spiritualistic explanation and felt that virtually all cases could be explained upon psychological and physiological grounds.

Emilio Servadio, born 1904. Psychoanalyst, parapsychologist. Dr. Servadio is a prominent Italian psychoanalyst who helped found the Italian Society for Psychical Research in 1937. He has written upon various facets of psi phenomena such as precognition, dowsing, dreams, and healing, but is especially concerned with telepathy and its relationship with psychoanalysis. His Myers Memorial Lecture in 1963 has been printed by the SPR and is an important discussion of psychosomatic and psi factors in healing, entitled *Unconscious and Paranormal Factors in Healing and Recovery.*

Eleanor M. B. Sidgwick, 1845-1936. Psychical researcher, educator, editor; President of the SPR, 1908-09. Mrs. Sidgwick, wife of Henry Sidgwick, sister of Arthur and Gerald Balfour, was a brilliant woman with a highly developed critical acumen, literary ability, and determination to investigate ostensible psi phenomena thoroughly. She was prominent in the SPR from the early 1880's until the 1930's and contributed greatly to its growth in prestige and to its accumulation of knowledge about paranormal phenomena. She studied many mediums, including Mrs. Piper, Mrs. Leonard, and Eusapia Palladino, and wrote numerous perceptive articles in the *Proceedings* of the PSR. While she doubted the survival hypothesis during a large part of her career, she was much impressed by the cross-correspondence material and indicated a few years before her death that she tended to accept that survival was a distinct possibility. Her writings even today are well worth study because of their acute analysis of the data, shrewd judgements of people and their motives, original hypotheses, and insistence upon objectivity.

Henry Sidgwick, 1838-1900. Philosopher, educator, founder of the SPR; President of the SPR, 1882-85, 1888-92. Sidgwick was the key figure in the founding of the SPR since many of the original members who responded to Barrett's call for such an organization agreed to its formation only if Sidgwick would act as President. His prestige, reputation for integrity, and brilliant abilities all attracted members of high repute and standing and helped set the tradition of excellence. He was a careful and skeptical investigator and took a leading part in the important Census of Hallucinations published in 1894, as well as studying the mediumship of Mrs. Piper, Eusapia Palladino, and others. His various Presidential Addresses remain important in shedding light upon the genesis of psychical research and in reminding the student of the remarkable consistency of the criticism and problems faced over ninety years by researchers.

S.G. Soal, born 1889. Mathematician, psychical researcher; President of the SPR, 1949-51. Dr. Soal has long been the most prominent statistical researcher in Great Britain. A distinguished academic mathematician and retired lecturer in mathematics at London University, he has brought to the statistical work an unusually strong knowledge of the mathematics of chance, as well as many years of study in psychical research. Before launching his statistical experiments, Dr. Soal spent some years investigating mediums and reported the very important Gordon Davis case in 1925. Through the mediumship of Mrs. Blanche Cooper, Soal received communications purporting to be from a friend, Gordon Davis, which were highly evidential, only to learn later that Davis was still alive. This pointed out, as did the Réallier case and some others, the highly developed dramatic faculty latent in mediums and the inherent difficulty, if not impossibility, of eliminating telepathy precognition, and/or clairvoyance (Super ESP hypothesis) as alternative explanations for ostensible discarnate sources of veridical data. Dr. Soal's most important work is doubtless his impressive statistical evidence for psi through a long series of experiments with Mrs. Stewart and Basil Shackleton. He undertook this work only after Whately Carington suggested that the displacement effect might be responsible for Soal's complete failure earlier to replicate Dr. Rhine's results. This proved to be true in the case of these two subjects, and in the new series extraordinary results were gained, especially by Shackleton, in precognitive tests. Besides numerous articles on psi, Dr. Soal's two most significant works are *Modern Experiments in Telepathy*, 1954, written with F. Bateman, and *The Mind Readers*, 1959, written with H.T. Bowden.

Ian Stevenson, born 1918. Professor of psychiatry, parapsychologist, physician. Dr. Stevenson has been especially concerned with the evidence for survival and for reincarnation, as well as the psychological concomitants of psi research and precognition. He has devised both a questionnaire and a padlock test for survival research which may shed light upon the Super ESP hypothesis and upon the nature of veridical survival evidence. Currently, he is probably the leading American parapsychologist working on the survival issue, after quite some years in which little attention was paid to this facet of psychical research. His principal publications have been *Twenty Cases Suggestive of Reincarnation*, 1966, and *Telepathic Impressions*, 1970.

W. H. C. Tenhaeff, born 1894. Parapsychologist, psychologist. Director of the Parapsychology Institute of the State University of Utrecht, Dr. Tenhaeff is the leading Dutch parapsychologist. While he has investigated virtually the entire spectrum of psi phenomena, his greatest interest in recent years has been in the study of the psychological characteristics of psychic sensitives. He has worked extensively with the well-known Dutch sensitive or "paragnost," Croiset, and has co-operated with researchers in other lands in the "chair tests" through which Croiset precognitively describes the person to sit in a particular chair at a given future date. These tests have provided some impressive instances of precognition. Dr. Tenhaeff has been exceedingly active in lecturing about parapsychology before a large number of organizations throughout Europe and has written many books upon different facets of psi phenomena.

C. *Drayton Thomas*, died 1953. Clergyman, psychical researcher. Rev. Thomas studied the mediumship of Mrs. Leonard more thoroughly than anyone, having had about five hundred sittings with her over thirty years. Convinced that he had received veridical communications from his father and sister as well as others, he was a leading survivalist. He helped devise the "book tests" and "newspaper tests," the former of a clairvoyant nature, the latter of a precognitive; and some of the results were impressive. While he disagreed with Whately Carington's conclusion that "Feda," Mrs. Leonard's control, was a secondary personality, he co-operated fully in the Word Association Tests to test this hypothesis. He wrote a considerable number of articles for the SPR about mediumship, proxy sittings, and various evidential cases; he also published several books embodying the results of his survival research. While other researchers did not share Thomas's conviction of survival, he was held in very high repute for his integrity and care in research.

Robert H. Thouless, born 1894. Psychologist, parapsychologist; President of the SPR, 1942-44. Dr. Thouless has concerned himself with PK research, statistical studies of ESP in the manner of Rhine and Soal, possibilities of improving guessing performance in such tests, and the issue of survival. In connection with the latter, he devised a complex cryptogram test for survival to obviate the drawbacks of the earlier posthumous tests, such as those of Myers and Lodge, which were useless once the key to the test had been used. Over the following years, he has refined this test and through this line of thought has engendered other survival tests, such as the padlock test of Dr. Ian Stevenson. He has written several articles about psi, and his book for laymen is an excellent contribution: *Experimental Psychical Research*, 1963.

H. C. Thurston, S. J., 1856-1939. Historian, priest, psychical researcher, writer. Probably the leading Roman Catholic expert upon psychical research, Father Thurston studied the field for thirty years. While he supported the Roman Catholic ban upon mediumistic contact with the discarnates and could not, therefore, study mediums firsthand, he was a close student of the literature and was in contact with some of the leading British researchers. Few have had a deeper knowledge of the evidence dealing with poltergeists. His principal work is *The Church and Spiritualism,* 1933, in which he disagreed with other Catholic writers that spiritualism was all fraud. This is a remarkably balanced and fair account of the movement as seen from the Roman Catholic viewpoint and remains an important contribution.

G. N. M. Tyrrell, 1879-1952. Engineer, mathematician, psychical researcher; President of the SPR 1945-46. Tyrrell, a pioneer in the development of radio, devoted his full time to psychical research for forty years. He became a leader in experimental work and also a prominent theoretician about psi. His devices for mechanical randomness and for testing both telepathy and precognition were significant developments; and through the use of these machines with Gertrude Johnson, he obtained highly significant statistical evidence for telepathy and precognition. Tyrrell wrote exceedingly well and brought his great knowledge and experience to bear upon the theoretical and philosophical meaning of psychical research in a series of very important works: *Grades of Significance*, 1930; *Science and Psychical Phenomena*, 1938; *The Personality of Man*, 1946; and *Human Personality*, 1953.

Montague Ullman, born 1916. Psychiatrist, parapsychologist. Dr. Ullman has been the leader in the field of dream research at the Dream Laboratory of Maimonides Hospital in New York. Here over almost a decade, he and his staff have studied telepathic exchange of ideas and images through dreaming, and they have greatly deepened the knowledge about the nature of dreams, the dramatic faculty of personality, and the different types of stimuli which seem to enhance telepathic rapport. He is currently the President of the ASPR, and recently returned from Russia where he learned about Russian parapsychological research.

L. L. Vasilyev, 1891-1966. Physiologist, parapsychologist. Vasilyev was the most prominent student of psi in Russia, established the first laboratory for parapsychological studies at Leningrad University, and urged that research into psi was a matter of the greatest importance. Like many physiologists and physicians in the field, he rejected the non-physicalistic properties of psi and insisted that it was an atavistic remainder from earlier forms of evolution which probably operated through some form of so far undiscovered energy in the brain. His most significant work is *Mysterious Manifestations of the Human Psyche,* 1959.

Margaret D. G. M. Verrall, 1859-1916. Classicist, automatist. Mrs. Verrall was the wife of a distinguished Cambridge classical scholar, A. W. Verrall, and a member of the Cambridge group of academic figures prominent in the SPR. She investigated both Mrs.

Thompson's and Mrs. Piper's mediumship before developing her own automatic writing. She was a leading member of the "SPR group" of automatists involved in the cross-correspondences, in the course of which she received veridical information purporting to originate with Frederic Myers, her husband, Henry Sidgwick, Richard Hodgson, and others. The complex and recondite classical allusions were typical of Myers, Verrall, Butcher and Sidgwick, but since she was herself a fine classicist, some students have argued that the cross-correspondences emanated from Mrs. Verrall's subconscious, telepathically triggering the jig-saw pieces found in the automatic writing of her daughter, Mrs. Piper, Mrs. Willett, Mrs. Forbes, and Mrs. Holland, although the mediums were as far apart as India and America. Mrs. Verrall was herself convinced of the discarnate source of the data.

Leslie D. Weatherhead, born 1893. Clergyman. One of the most famous preachers and religious authors in the world, Dr. Weatherhead has long been interested in psychical research, especially in healing and survival. He has argued that knowledge of so-called paranormal phenomena sheds light upon the numerous similar instances in the Bible, upon the resurrection, and upon the nature of miracles. He has written several books upon facets of psychical research, including *The Resurrection of Christ in the Light of Modern Science and Psychical Research*, 1959, but his major work is the massive volume, *Psychology, Religion, and Healing*, 1951.

CHAPTER SEVEN

GLOSSARY OF TERMS

The definitions of those terms marked with * are used with the permission of and through the kindness of the Editor of *The Journal of Parapsychology*.

Agent: The "sender" in tests for telepathy, the person whose mental states are to be apprehended by the percipient. In GESP tests, the person who looks at the target object.

Apparition: An hallucination with some paranormal cause. Some students hold that some apparitions have a spatial reality, but most researchers feel that an apparition is an exteriorized hallucination corresponding to some veridical person or occurrence and caused by some psi linkage. The process or psychologically triggered mechanism involved is not known, although various theories have been advanced, principally by Myers and Tyrrell.

Apport: An object which appears at seances, ostensibly by means of penetration of matter, i.e., an object is "dematerialized," transported through intervening material obstacles such as walls, and "rematerialized" in its original form. The evidence for apports under anything like satisfactory controls is very scanty, and known fraudulent instances have been numerous. Most apports are small objects like stones, but live animals, plants, and flowers have also appeared. This phenomenon is much more rare today than in the heyday of physical mediumship.

Astral Body: Also frequently termed "etheric body." Said to be an exact, non-physical replica of the individual physical body which separates at death and occasionally before death. According to spiritualists and theosophists it is the vehicle for the spirit in the first state after death and is sometimes faintly perceived as apparitions, phantasms, ghosts, or haunts.

Astral Projection: See *Out-of-the-Body Experience.*

Automatic Writing: Writing done in a dissociated state of varying degree. The writing is done without conscious muscular effort or mental direction.

*BT (Basic Technique): The clairvoyance technique in which each card is laid aside by the experimenter as it is called by the subject. The check-up is made at the end of the run.

Cabinet: An enclosed space, generally surrounded by curtains, often no more than a curtain drawn across a corner of a room, which physical mediums claim they need in order that they can concentrate or condense the "psychic force" or energy by means of which they perform ostensible materializations, raps, etc. Some mediums sit within the cabinet, others at the entrance, while a few, notably D. D. Home, have dispensed with one.

Call: The subject's guess (or cognitive response) in trying to identify the target in an ESP test.

Chance: The complex of undefined causal factors irrelevent to the purpose at hand.

Mean Chance Expectation (also *Chance Expectation* and *Chance Average*): The most likely score if only chance is involved.

Chi-Square: A sum of quantities, each of which is a deviation squared divided by an expected value. Also a sum of the squares of CR's (q.v.).

Circle: A group sitting with a medium, generally in a circle, possibly holding hands or with knees touching, or both, the reason given being that this establishes an ostensible "psychic current" which can be utilized by the medium and/or discarnates for paranormal manifestations. *A Circle for Development* or *Development Circle* is one which meets for the purpose of leading to the improvement and growth of mediumistic powers among the members, under the guidance of an acknowledged medium.

Clairaudience: Extrasensory data perceived as sound. Generally considered a facet of clairvoyance.

Clairsentience: Extrasensory data perceived as heightened feeling or awareness. Generally considered a facet of clairvoyance. Sometimes also termed *Telaesthesia.*

Clairvoyance: Extrasensory perception of objects or objective events.

Communicator: A purported discarnate personality, or surviving personality of a deceased individual, which manifests through a medium.

Control: A personality or purported discarnate entity which frequently or regularly seems to take control of the medium during trance. An example is Mrs. Leonard's control Feda. Also used for any personality controlling or directing the speech and/or actions of the medium.

CR (Critical Ratio): A measure to determine whether or not the observed deviation is significantly greater than the expected random fluctuation about the average. The CR is obtained by dividing the observed deviation by the standard deviation. (The probability of a given CR may be obtained by consulting tables of the probability integral, such as Pearson's.)

Cross Correspondences: A highly complex series of mediumistic records, in the form of automatic writings and speech, which have been shown to fit into exceedingly recondite patterns of veridical information, principally dealing with classical allusions. The plan for such puzzles purportedly originated with the early leader of the Society for Psychical Research, F. W. H. Myers, after his death, to demonstrate survival by eliminating "telepathic leakage," i.e., the medium's tapping of the sitter's mind by telepathy, as a possible explanation for veridical information which seemed to come from a discarnate. Bits of information, clues, and hints, meaningless in themselves, were received by several automatists as far apart as India, America, and Great Britain, within brief periods of time, often containing references to the other automatists concerned, and purporting to originate with the discarnate Myers and/or several other deceased former leaders of the Society for Psychical Research. The numerous pieces of the puzzles had to be fit together into a meaningful whole by investigators, one of whom, Alice Johnson, was the first to notice the corresponding references among the scripts. The painstaking and most scholarly study of the *Cross Correspondences* was carried on for many years and covers many hundreds of pages in the *Proceedings* of the Society for Psychical Research. The most recent case of this type, "The Palm Sunday Case," a most impressive instance, was first published in 1960. Many students consider the *Cross Correspondences* the most impressive evidence yet obtained in support of the *Dualist Hypothesis* (q.v.)

Cryptothesia: Older term for *General Extrasensory Perception* (*GESP*) (q.v.).

Crystal Gazing: See *Scrying.*

*Deviation: The amount an observed number of hits or an average score varies (either above or below) from mean chance expectation of a run or series or other unit of trials.

*Differential Effect: Significant difference between scoring rates when subjects are participating in an experiment in which two procedural conditions (such as two types of targets or two modes of response) are compared.

Direct Voice: An ostensibly paranormal isolated voice without any apparent source. Most frequently manifested through a small "trumpet" or megaphone by a physical medium, it is rare today. It was often shown to be fraudulent, and the evidence for the phenomenon under controlled conditions is sparse.

Discarnate: Disembodied. Used in mediumistic communications to refer to the surviving personality of a deceased person. The term implies that the surviving personality no longer has a "body" in any physical sense of the word.

*Displacement: ESP responses to targets other than those for which the calls were intended.

Backward Displacement: ESP reponses to targets

preceding the intended targets. Displacement to the targets one, two, three, etc. places preceding the intended target are designated as (-1), (-2), (-3), etc.

Forward Displacement: ESP responses to targets coming later than the intended targets. Displacement to the targets one, two, three, etc. places after the intended target are designated as (+1), (+2), (+3), etc.

Dissociation: Division of the mind or personality with one or more parts behaving as if independent of the rest.

DT (Down Through): The clairvoyance technique in which the cards are called down through the pack before any are removed or checked.

Dowsing: The apparent ability of some people to locate water, minerals, or objects through the use of a V-shaped "dowsing rod," most often of wood, but frequently of metal or other materials. When the two ends of the rod are held with the apex pointing outwards from the dowser, it is claimed that the apex will dip and point to the ground over the water or other object sought. Some dowsers have used pendulums, and some claim success through using the rod or pendulum merely over a map of the area concerned. The evidence that some dowsers are successful in locating water, minerals, pipes, electrical conduits, etc. far more often than could reasonably be attributed to chance is quite strong; many commercial firms have paid considerable fees for their services and have vouched for the success of the dowser. Whether dowsing is paranormal, however, is a matter of considerable controversy among psychical researchers. Some have held that the dowser clairvoyantly perceives the object of the search, and involuntary muscular action then dips the rod; others that success is due to shrewd knowledge of topography, and that failures are forgotten or ignored.

Dualist Hypothesis: The tentative view that the psi faculty is non-physical in nature, demonstrating that the human mind, at least in part, is non-physical, and could, therefore, theoretically, survive the physical dissolution of the body and brain at death; also that a surviving discarnate mind or personality or fragment of such might be able to communicate through and, on occasion, control a medium, and is therefore responsible for some paranormal veridical information or other phenomena produced. It should be noted that many who have held this view have not been *Spiritualists* (q.v.). The principal distinctions are that the dualist holds this standpoint as a working hypothesis with which to examine the data, not as a religious belief, and would generally consider the hypothesis as applicable only in cases where other paranormal sources, such as ESP, precognition, or PK, could be eliminated. The spiritualist, on the other hand, has tended to accept discarnate origin and control for a much larger proportion of paranormal phenomena.

Ectoplasm: Term introduced by Charles Richet to describe the "exteriorized substance" ostensibly emitted by some physical mediums through various bodily orifices. From ectoplasm, it was claimed, faces, limbs, and even full figures of discarnate personalities were formed and recognized by relatives as life-like in appearance. Darkness has been said to be essential as the substance is sensitive to light. This has made fraud easy, and many exposures of "ectoplasm" as muslin and other substances have been made. Conversely, some highly trained and critical experts like Richet and Geley were utterly convinced that they had obtained irrefutable evidence for ectoplasms under the most rigidly controlled laboratory conditions. Manifestations are extremely rare today.

Extended Telepathy: See *Super ESP.*

*ESP *(Estrasensory Perception):* Experience of, or response to, a target object, state, event, or influence without sensory contact.

*ESP *Cards:* Cards, each bearing one of the following five symbols: star, circle, square, cross, and waves (three parallel wavy lines). A standard pack has 25 cards.

Closed Pack: An ESP pack composed of five each of the five symbols.

Open Pack: An ESP pack made up of the ESP symbols selected in random order.

Expectation: See *Chance.*

Extrachance: Not due to chance alone.

Foreknowledge: See *Precognition.*

*GESP *(General Extrasensory Perception):* ESP which could be either telepathy or clairvoyance or both.

Ghost: See *Apparition.* As popularly utilized, this term denotes only the apparition of a deceased person, and is not sufficiently precise for use in psychical research.

Hallucination: Experiencing or perceiving sensory data which have no physical or objective case; e.g., "seeing" a table that is not there spatially.

Veridical Hallucination: An hallucination corresponding with some degree of accuracy to an external object, person, or event, but *not* caused by that object, person, or event directly.

Haunt: Ostensibly paranormal phenomena seemingly connected with a certain location, especially a building. The reported phenomena have included apparitions, poltergeist manifestations, cold draughts, sounds of steps and voices, and various odors.

Hit: A correct response in a test for some facet of psi or PK.

Illusion: An erroneous interpretation of sensory data actually obtained normally; e.g., mistaking a tall bush waving in the wind for the figure of a person.

Levitation: The purported rising into the air of persons or objects without any apparent agency as required by known physical laws of motion and gravity. There are numerous well-attested instances of this phenomenon, some under excellent conditions. As the statistical evidence for PK has grown, the evidence for the possibility of levitation theoretically has also been strengthened, but reports of levitation today are extremely rare.

*MCE (Mean Chance Expectation): See *Chance.*

Medium: A person who perceives, communicates, and/or demonstrates ostensibly paranormal phenomena regularly and/or with some degree of ability to do so at will. A term less favored by psychical researchers than "sensitive" or "psychic," since "medium" implies a "go-between" and is used by spiritualists to indicate the person acting as a means of communicating with purported surviving discarnate personalities.

Miss: An erroneous response in a test for some facet of psi or PK.

Ouija Board: From "oui" and "ja," meaning "yes" in French and German. A wooden board with letters and numerals arranged in crescent shapes, it is used with a tripod at whose apex is a pointer. When one or more persons place their fingers lightly upon the pointer it spells out "messages" by stopping at letters. Some important cases in psychical research have begun with paranormal information coming through the ouija board, e.g., Mrs. Curran and "Patience Worth." Unquestionably, much, if not all, of the material is derived from the subconscious of the operator(s) who unconsciously directs the pointer. Some students have held, however, that there is evidence of discarnate influence or direction. Many researchers have pointed out the inherent dangers of using the ouija board or of taking its "messages" seriously, because of the possibility of dredging up some very unpleasant and potentially disturbing attitudes and facts from one's subconscious. There have been numerous instances of persons who have become very upset emotionally from the use of the ouija board.

Ostensible: Seeming; indicating that there is the possibility of paranormal causation or of a paranormal factor being present, but that such causation or factor has not been conclusively demonstrated.

Out-of-the-Body Experience: Also frequently termed "astral travel" or "astral projection." The purported detachment, voluntary or involuntary, of the *Astral Body* (q.v.) from the phsyical body, the two generally remaining connected by a distended "cord." In this state of "projection," percipients have claimed to perceive their physical body lying inert, to see and hear people while reamaining imperceptible themselves, to perceive and remember people, places, objects, and occurrences which were beyond the reach of their physical senses. While there are excellent cases of ostensible astral projection which demonstrate paranormal perception or veridical information, many researchers would hold that ESP can account for the data, while the experience itself of astral projection would be hallucinatory in nature.

*P (Probability): A mathematical estimate of the expected

frequency of a given result or set of results from chance alone.

Paranormal: Generally synonymous with *Parapsychical* (q.v.). Refers to those faculties and phenomena which are beyond "normality" in terms of cause and effect as currently understood.

Parapsychical (Parapsychological): Attributable to psi.

Parapsychology: The branch of science that deals with psi communication, i.e., behavioral or personal exchanges with the environment which are extrasensorimotor— not dependent on the senses and muscles.

Percipient: The person experiencing ESP; also one who is tested for ESP ability.

Phantasm: See *Apparition.*

PK (Psychokinesis): The extramotor aspect of psi; a direct (i.e., mental but non-muscular) influence exerted by the subject on an external physical process, condition, or object.

Placement Test: A PK technique in which the aim of the subject is to try to influence falling objects to come to rest in a designated area of the throwing surface.

Planchette: A *Ouija Board* pointer with a pen or pencil thrust through the apex. The operator then allows the planchette to write "messages" by placing the fingers lightly upon it as it glides over the paper. See *Ouija Board.*

Poltergeist: Literally "noisy spirit." Termed *Recurrent Spontaneous Psychokinesis (RSPK)* by some modern researchers, the ostensibly paranormal manifestations include the throwing, lifting, and breaking of objects, the setting of fires, and, occasionally, personal injuries to people involved. There is very frequently a child near puberty at the center of the activity. While many cases have been shown by researchers to be fraudulent or attributable to natural causes, there are some very well-attested instances of clearly paranormal phenomena of the poltergeist type.

Precognition: Prediction of random future events, the occurrence of which cannot be inferred from present knowledge.

*Preferential Matching: A method of scoring responses to free material. A judge ranks the stimulus objects (usually pictures in sets of four) with respect to their similarity to, or association with, each response; and/or he ranks the responses with respect to their similarity to, or association with, each stimulus object.

Preternatural: An older term for *Paranormal* (q.v.).

Proxy Sitting: A sitting at which the sitter acts as a substitute for someone in attempting to obtain paranormal information through the medium. There have been instances where the proxy sitter did not even know the name of the person for whom he was sitting. This helps eliminate "telepathic leakage" from the sitter as a possible source of any veridical information furnished by the medium.

Psi: The general term for extrasensory perception and extrasensorimotor activity. *Psi* includes telepathy, clairvoyance, precognition, retrocognition, and pyschokinesis.

*Psi Missing: Exercise of psi ability in a way that avoids the target the subject is attempting to hit.

Psi Phenomena: Occurrences resulting from the operation of *Psi* .

Psychic: A general adjectival term for paranormal events, abilities, studies, etc. Also a synonym for *Sensitive* or *Medium* (q.v.).

Psychic Photography: See *Spirit Photography*.

Psychical Research: Generally synonymous with *Para-*

psychology (q.v.), this is the name for the study of paranormal phenomena and the psi faculty originally used and still widely utilized, especially outside of the United States.

Psychometry: The technique of obtaining ostensibly paranormal information through touching or handling an object. Generally considered a facet of clairvoyance, many students would consider that the object touched acts as a focal point or catalyst psychologically for the exercise of the psi faculty, much as a crystal ball does in *Scrying* (q.v.). Many mediums, however, consider that there is a "psychic residue" upon the object, collected during its use and available through psychic touch and clairvoyance to give veridical information about the person who owned or used the object.

Purported, Purporting: See *Ostensible.*

RSPK (Recurrent Spontaneous Psychokinesis): See *Poltergeist.*

Retrocognition: Paranormal knowledge of past events beyond the range of inference or memory on the part of the subject.

*Run: A group of trials, usually the successive calling of a deck of 25 ESP cards or symbols. In PK tests, 24 single die-throws regardless of the number of dice thrown at the same time.

*Score: The number of hits made in any given unit of trials, usually a run.

Script: An example of *Automatic Writing* (q.v.) or of a record of automatic speech.

Scrying: Also termed *Crystal Gazing.* A technique of focussing the psi faculty, especially *Clairvoyance* (q.v.) by staring into a crystal ball, pool of water, coffee grounds, tea leaves, or like focal point; this seemingly may act upon the psi faculty and cause pictures, sometimes of veridical data, to form a type of exteriorized hallucination. In all probability, the staring induces a type of dissociation which aids in the exercise of the psi faculty.

*SD (Standard Deviation): Usually the theoretical root mean square of the deviations. It is obtained from the formula $\sqrt{npq}$ in which *n* is the number of single trials, *p* the probability of success per trial, and *q* the probability of failure.

Seance: A *sitting* (q.v.), generally of a group of six to ten persons.

Second Sight: A term used in Celtic folklore, especially, for ostensibly paranormal ability, possibly of the psi faculty.

Sensitive: Medium (q.v.). Preferred by many psychical researchers because it does not have the implications of acceptance of the spiritist hypothesis which the term *Medium* has.

*Series: Several runs of experimental sessions that are grouped in accordance with the stated purpose and design of the experiment.

*Set: A subdivision of the record page serving as a scoring unit for a consecutive group of trials, usually for the same target.

*Significance: A numerical result is significant when it equals or surpasses some criterion of degree of chance improbability. The criterion commonly used in parapsychology today is a probability value of .02 (odds of 50 to 1 against change) or less, or a deviation in either direction such that the CR is 2.33 or greater. Odds of 20 to 1 (probability of .05) are regarded as strongly suggestive.

*Singles Test: A PK technique in which the aim of the subject is to try to influence dice to fall with a specified face up.

Sitting: A session with a medium, generally by an individual, or a small number of persons.

STM (Screened Touch Matching): An ESP card-testing technique in which the subject indicates in each trial (by pointing to one of five key positions) what he thinks the top card is in the inverted pack held by the experimenter behind a screen. The card is then laid opposite that position.

Spirit Photography: The purported photographing of the faces or forms of discarnate spirits, called "extras," upon photographs otherwise taken normally and ostensibly upon a plate or film which has not been tampered with in any way to produce such "extras." Also termed *Psychic Photography*, it flourished in the late nineteenth century and the first third of this century. A great many spirit photographers were exposed as fraudulent, and the evidence for the genuineness of this phenomenon as paranormal under controlled conditions is very slight.

Spiritualism: The religious movement which holds that: (1) man's personality (spirit) survives death as a *Discarnate* (q.v.); (2) discarnates can and do demonstrate this individual survival by communications of veridical information and by physical manifestations such as raps, apparitions, poltergeist activity, and materializations, generally through psychically gifted individuals termed *Mediums* (q.v.) who act as vehicles or communication between the two spheres of existence; (3) man's individual survival as a self-conscious, idiosyncratic, remembering personality can thus be an empirically proven fact, and not merely a hopeful article of faith.

Spiritualist: A follow of *Spiritualism* (q.v.).

Spontaneous Phenomena: See *Spontaneous Psi Experience.*

Spontaneous Psi Experience: Natural, unplanned occurrence of an event or experience that seems to involve
   parapsychical ability.

Subject: The person who is tested in an experiment.

Subliminal: Beneath the "threshold" of consciousness.

Super ESP Hypothesis: The hypothesis that any veridical
   information is theoretically available to the percipient
   via telepathy, clairvoyance, precognition, or
   retrocognition, and, therefore, to postulate a discarnate
   source, as the spiritist hypothesis does, is unnecessary
   and, therefore, unjustifiable as an additional assump-
   tion to explain the paranormally obtained information.
   Since there are no known limits to the psi faculties, any
   human knowledge, even if only in someone's subconscious, any extant document or object may be
   accessible to the percipient; thus, if the information is
   verifiable as veridical, it is theoretically possible that
   the percipient could obtain the information by means
   of the exercise of *Super ESP.* Until such a possibility
   can be eliminated, the *dualist hypothesis* is not the
   most parsimonious explanation, and should be rejected
   in favor of the *Super ESP Hypothesis.* Some students,
   however, hold that in the cases of the most impressive
   mediumistic data, such as the *Cross Correspondences*
   (q.v.), the instantaneous selection of pertinent data
   from the billions of potentially available items, and the
   construction of a realistic, idiosyncratic personality
   with the proper characteristics to impress the highly
   critical investigators concerned presupposes a range,
   power, and sophistication of exercise of the psi faculty
   far beyond that for which there is any other evidence.
   They hold, therefore, that the *Super ESP Hypothesis* is
   not so direct or parsimonious as the *dualist hypothesis.*

Supernormal: See *Paranormal. Paranormal* is preferred by

psychical researchers since it does not imply that the faculties or phenomena in this category are in any sense superior to other faculties or phenomena, merely different and not currently congruent with known norms of causation or behaviour.

Supraliminal: Above the threshold of consciousness.

Survival Hypothesis: See *Dualist Hypothesis.*

Table Tipping: Also termed "Table turning." A method of receiving "messages" purportedly from discarnates. Sitters place their hands lightly on the table and by levitation and tapping the table spells out the messages by giving a rap with a leg when the sitters come to the relevant letter of the alphabet as they repeat the alphabet aloud.

*Target: In ESP tests, the objective or mental events to which the subject is attempting to respond; in PK tests, the objective process or object which the subject tries to influence (such as the face or location of a die).

Target Card: The card which the precipient is attempting to identify or otherwise indicate a knowledge of.

Target Face: The face of the falling die which the subject tries to make turn by the PK.

Target Pack: The pack of cards the order of which the subject is attempting to identify.

Telaesthesia: An older term for *Clairvoyance* or *Clairsentience* (q.v.).

Telekinesis: An older term for PK (*Psychokinesis*) (q.v.).

*Telepathy: Extrasensory perception of the mental state or activity of another person.

Trance: A state of psychological dissociation varying in degree of depth among mediums. Generally self-induced.

Travelling Clairvoyance: The paranormal perception of

persons, events, objects, or places by ostensibly "travelling" to another location psychically while remaining in the present location physically. Often practiced under hypnosis *or* self-induced trance, it is not to be confused with *Astral Travel* (q.v.). The percipients have sometimes given strikingly veridical data. The percipient's sense of being "there" while his body remained "here" would generally be regarded as a veridical hallucination, as he paranormally perceived the veridical items via some aspect of the psi faculty.

*Trial: In ESP tests, a single attempt to identify a target object; in PK tests, a single unit of effect to be measured in the evaluation of results.

Veridical: Corresponding to or conveying fact. Utilized with reference to items obtained paranormally which have been verified. See especially its use in connection with *Hallucination* (q.v.).